CW01511026

WHEN
LIFE
IS
FULL
OF
IT

AN ANTIDOTE FOR YOUR MIND

STAN BELYSHEV

ISBN: 9781982962654 (Paperback)
ASIN: B07D283HL7 (Kindle)

NextGen Leaders Academy

www.StanBelyshev.com

Printed in the United States of America

CONTENTS

INTRODUCTION

Contents

WARNING!

> *"Our world is already full of it, so please*
> *do not be a contributor!"*
> —Stan Belyshev

INTRODUCTION

I would love to dedicate this book to everyone who understands that *life is full of it*! To everyone who still has breath in their nostrils; to mothers and fathers; to young and old; to the brave and to the cowards; to dummies and to the nerds; to entrepreneurs and business owners; to mothers-in-law and mother outlaws; to the executives and the janitors; to the government and the military personnel; to the legal or illegal immigrants; to the religious and to the atheists; to the hopeful, joyful or brokenhearted; to the penniless and the wealthy; to the circumcised or uncircumcised; to the single, married or divorced! And if you're not one of those who comes across the understanding that *life is full of it*, then you must be God, because even the lovable Mother Teresa faced enormous problems and setbacks on a daily basis.

Warning, this book is not intended to tickle your selfish ego with more motivational encouragements, give you an essential oil massage or to give you simple principles on changing your attitude so you can claim your participation trophy at the end. Heck no! My goal is to slap you with a reality check of common sense by throwing you into the boot camp called *LIFE*! And with that said, *life* can be defined in a short sentence: *It's not what happens; it's what you do with it."*

It's no secret that *life is full of it*. But the truth is that you are responsible for your life and how you deal with your everyday issues. Life is full of problems, but problems come and go. Life is full of challenges and obstacles, but you are able to maneuver through and overcome those challenges. Life is full of pain, but you are able to endure the pain and eventually recover. Life is full of evil and darkness, but you carry an inner light of hope and courage with which you can influence others. Life is full of broken families and divorces, but you are able to recover, to restore and to start all over again. Life is full of criticism, but the truth is that you can use it as stepping stones to move forward. Life is full of financial challenges and crisis, but you are more than able to recover and to excel further. Life is full of broken promises and betrayal, but you can still model integrity, honesty and accountability. And life is full of uncertainty, but you can choose to stay optimistic and focused on your dreams and goals.

How It All Began

When Life Is Full of It, requires a little boldness on my part, but with minimal risk. Allow me to give you a quick introduction of how this book was originally conceived.

During one of the most challenging seasons of my life, when just about everything came crashing down, I was forced to take a second job as truck driver delivering expedited products all over the nation. It's one thing to deliver regular products, but it's a whole different ballgame when the product needs to be delivered one business day after the order is placed. The job itself seemed laid back, but the drivers were deprived of sleep, broke many regulations by driving longer hours, and had an unhealthy junk-food diet, since truck stops were our primary source of food.

When I started, I had to drive an older truck that gave me many issues on the road. One day it quit on me in the heat of Texas. Due to some mechanical technicalities in the truck, I was stranded for about three days while it was being fixed. And to make things worse, I wasn't able to get a hotel, so I slept for two nights on the carpeted floor of the local truck shop. Of course, all of these things combined fired me up and the needle of my personal stress-o-meter was buried in the red zone.

After I broke the news to my wife, we were both upset, since I wasn't going to be home when I'd planned, and wasn't making any money while the truck was being fixed. As I lay there on that hard, carpeted floor in genuine frustration, I began to reevaluate my life. A thought hit me: *Life is full of it.* As I lay there, the thought kept growing, like a rolling snowball, until I began to ask myself a series of questions.

Is my situation a tombstone or a stepping stone?
Is this a problem or an opportunity?
Am I getting bitter or better?
Is this a trial in my life or a triumphant moment?
Am I going to complain about my situation or contain it?

Eventually, I began to have a serious conversation with myself. At that moment, I had an epiphany. I jumped up from the floor, grabbed a pen and a notepad from my computer bag, and began to write. And during those three backbreaking nights, I poured out everything that was being downloaded into my heart and mind. As you read these pages, you'll be diving into a detailed outline of unique individuals who had to readjust their mental attitudes when hardship struck—but in that process, their names have become well known around the world.

We all go through various life moments; I'm sure many of you have your own books that you could write about this. With that said, I want to encourage you, my friend, to devote yourself to the continual progression of working with your attitude on a daily basis, as you *grow* through life, not just *go* through life. Enjoy this process, since it will be a life-long journey.

Attitude is a mindset, which means you need to set your mind in a specific way of thinking. The challenging part about this is that this is not a one-time process, but a continual practice, since we are bombarded on a daily basis with various challenges, obstacles, problems and personal issues. Your attitude also determines your mental conditioning. Just as our bodies require daily food for nourishment, we need to feed our attitudes with the right discipline and the right perspective of life.

While you read this book, you will be encouraged; you will be challenged; you will be motivated; you will be smacked with a reality check; you might feel rebuked; and in some chapters you may even want to hit me or throw the book against the wall (Hopefully you won't do that with your Kindle reader!). But nevertheless you will not be the same, since you will be introduced to several individuals who had the right mental attitude in their lives and as a result, have changed the lives of millions and even transformed our modern society.

I have purposefully outlined thirty-one chapters, which you can use as a type of a devotional for each day of the month. Every chapter will contain a unique real life situation or situations and how your attitude responds or reacts to them. And hopefully, you will be able to take in a full dose of positive mental attitude, as it begins to transform your thinking, just like an antidote would!

Chapter 1

WHEN LIFE IS FULL OF

IT

An Antidote For Your Mind

Every day we are faced with various choices and decisions; the choices we make will determine the outcome. Life doesn't come to us on a silver platter with golden spoons and forks to feast with; it comes to all of us full of surprises, setbacks and even heartaches.

The Bible says the tongue is a little member of our body, but can boast great things. And this same tongue is like a little flame that can eventually set a whole forest on fire. Furthermore, we're told, mankind has the ability to tame many animals, but no man can ever tame the tongue. With it we praise and encourage others and with it we likewise curse and degrade others.

How amazing is it that in one moment we can express pleasant words and in the next breath we can tell someone off! In one moment we praise our children with a smile on our faces, but a moment later we are screaming at them at the top of our lungs! Even nature can speak volumes to us all about this: An apple tree can only reproduce apples and a strawberry field can only reproduce strawberries; hopefully the cow continues to give us milk and not orange juice. But we as human beings are capable of so many unpredictable things.

For example, what we feel, we will say and express; what we like or don't like will eventually be known by others; the discomfort or trials we go through, we make known to all of our friends and family members. And the list just goes on!

This brings me to my final thought: A bad attitude is like foul breath. We know we have it, but we have become immune to its smell. Just because we are not annoyed by it does not mean that others won't squirm or have watery eyes. And you can be ignorant about how annoyed or uncomfortable others may feel around you.

Antidote For Your Mind

While you can't always change what's going on around you, you do have the power to change what's going on within you. For example, when life throws a pile of crap at you, just turn it into fertilizer and use it to fertilize your future attitude crops! When life gives you sour lemons, add some water and sugar and turn it into lemonade! When life throws you a curve ball, be ready to swing. That way, you won't be standing idle, and taking one strike after another.

Here's something else to think about. Gloves keep your hands warm in the winter cold! Sunscreen protects your skin from being burnt by the sun! An umbrella keeps you dry from the rain! Seatbelts and airbags provide a higher percentage of safety during a car crash. In the same way, your attitude can either protect you or expose you; guide you or misdirect you; and become your best friend or your worst enemy.

One of the main focuses of this reality-check book is for us to stop complaining about our problems and issues and simply enjoy life to its fullest. Remember, the world is already full of it, and we don't need another contributor.

What is Attitude?

- *Attitude* will determine your approach to life.
- *Attitude* will determine your relationships with others.
- *Attitude* will show the difference between your successes or failures.
- *Attitude* will determine whether you soar like an eagle or walk around like a chicken.
- *Attitude* will determine your level of integrity and honesty.
- *Attitude* will reflect how far you are willing to compromise.
- *Attitude* will determine your level of discipline and accountability.
- *Attitude* will open or close doors of opportunities.
- *Attitude* will determine the type of friends you will have.
- *Attitude* will expose your true inner character.
- *Attitude* will determine how you will respond or react to critics and criticism.
- *Attitude* will determine whether you will manage others or be led by them.
- *Attitude* will determine the vision you will have for your life.

• *Attitude* will determine the culture that you create around yourself.

• *Attitude*, like a compass, will determine how you know which direction you're headed in your life's journey.

• *Attitude* will determine whether you are a leader or a follower.

• *Attitude* will determine who you will attract or repel.

• *Attitude* is be never content until it is expressed.

• *Attitude* is the librarian of your past, the speaker of your present, and the prophet of your future.

THE BIRTH OF YOUR ATTITUDE

Again, what is attitude? Attitude is your inward core beliefs, which then affect your feelings, your outlook, your actions, and is eventually expressed by behavior. Attitude starts as a tiny seed in your mind, which slowly begins to sprout as it breaks out of its shell and begins to spread its roots into your thought process. And your attitude will determine whether you give root to a strong redwood or a thorny bush. So your attitude, whether positive or negative, feeds this seed like fertilizer.

People often have wrong beliefs about attitude, which they try to hide behind or use to justify their behaviors. For example, they would say:

- I was born with this *attitude.*
- I received this *attitude* from my mother, my father, my grandfather or from my grandmother.
- My *attitude* will naturally adjust as I get older.
- I can't help it, it's how my *attitude* is.
- Well, this is my *attitude*, take it or leave it.

No matter what reason or excuse you use to cover up your nasty attitude, the reality is this: You are responsible for your attitude no matter what! The thirty-one practical life principles you'll find discussed throughout this book are not meant to give you a sugar high or a short-term energy boost. Rather, think of them as daily vitamins for your heart, your mind, your body, and your soul.

Chapter 2
<u>TOMBSTONE OR STEPPING STONE?</u>

Live Your Life With Purpose

The easiest choices are always to bury our problems and disappointments in life. Yes, life will come hard at you like a Mack truck and won't apologize, but how you respond or react will determine if you are going to bury yourself or use that as an opportunity to move forward.

As the saying goes, "Grass is always greener on the other side of the fence." But have you ever considered that your neighbor may have some major problems, too? Yes, much of life can be evaluated through simple comparison. If you think you have it tough in your life, then just look around or even ask your neighbors, and you will definitely find at least one individual who is going through greater hell than you are.

So before you start to complain about your problems, know there are many people out there who have it much tougher than you. Plenty of stones will be thrown at you throughout your life, but what you do with them is a choice: You can make them your tombstone—or a stepping stone to something greater.

As we dive through the pages of history, we come across phenomenal patriarchs who have shaped societies and laid out plenty of stepping stones for us to walk upon.

THE LIFE ATTITUDE OF ABRAHAM LINCOLN

Abraham Lincoln is considered to be one of America's greatest presidents, but without a doubt he also had his humble beginnings. When Abraham Lincoln was seven years old, his family was forced out of their home and he had to go to work to help support them. When he was twenty-two, his business failed. When he was twenty-three, he ran for state legislature and lost, the race, as well as the job he held at the time. At age twenty-four, he borrowed some money from a friend to begin a business and by the end of the year was bankrupt. He spent the next seventeen years paying off this debt.

When he was twenty-six, he was engaged to be married, but his sweetheart died and his heart was broken. When he was twenty-seven, he had a total nervous breakdown and was bedridden for six months. At age twenty-nine, he sought to become speaker of the state House of Representatives, but was defeated. At thirty-one, he desired to become a member of the Electoral College, but was defeated. At age thirty-two, he ran for Congress and lost.

When he was 40, he sought the job of land officer in his home state, but was rejected. When he was forty-five, he ran for a seat in the U.S. Senate and lost. When he was forty-seven, he sought the vice presidential nomination at the Republican National Convention and got less than one hundred votes. When he was forty-nine he ran for U.S. Senate again—and lost again.

But in 1860, at the age of fifty-one Abraham Lincoln was elected president of the United States.

Lincoln's presidency was not smooth sailing either, since he had a passionate belief that all slaves should be set free. And in 1863, he released the Emancipation Proclamation, declaring more than three million enslaved people were now free. This eventually gave birth to the American Civil War. Later that year, Lincoln announced that Thanksgiving would be a national holiday.

Abraham Lincoln is recognized as one of our country's greatest presidents, but from time to time he struggled with depression and thoughts of suicide. He faced a fair share of opposition from his own party members, but that did not stop him from achieving historical significance before being assassinated by well-known stage actor John Wilkes Booth on April 14, 1865.

Abraham Lincoln can definitely teach us valuable life lessons about using our obstacles, challenges and closed doors as stepping stones to create a path that will lead us closer to our purpose and destiny. Lincoln summed up his own life with the words, "Nearly all men can stand adversity, but if you want to test a man's character, give him power."

Attitude Principles To Consider

- Never give up or give in, no matter how many times you are rejected.
- It's a fact that you will fail at times, but failure will never define who you truly are.
- If a common person can achieve great success, then there is hope for you.
- Your concern should never be with your failure—only whether you are content with that failure.

- Start preparing yourself today, since you will never know when your moment to shine will come.
- If you are not wiser today than you were yesterday, you are not growing.
- Occasional defeat in life is inevitable, but success is irresistible.
- Don't be quick to make enemies, but be wise and patient enough to turn your enemies into friends.
- You can only be as happy as you make up your mind to be.
- Be prepared. Lincoln once said, "Give me six hours to chop down a tree, and I will spend the first four hours sharpening the axe."

Lincoln's attitude was to never give up, no matter the cost. He is one of my personal heroes; his portrait hangs behind my desk on my office wall, to continually remind me that he lived a life of purpose and has laid out plenty of stepping stones for me to walk upon.

Attitude Questions To Consider

1. **Are you collecting stepping stones or building a tombstone?**
2. **Are you planning on living or existing?**
3. **What price are you willing to pay for your success?**

Chapter 3
PROBLEM OR OPPORTUNITY?

You Were Born to Solve Something Specific

The World's Only Monument Dedicated To A Pest

I found this unique story to be amazing. In Alabama, there stands the world's only monument dedicated to a destructive pest, the Boll Weevil. In a nutshell, this small beetle brought much destruction to the cotton industry back in the 1930s, destroying about 60 percent of the Alabama's crop in one year. The cotton farmers frantically tried to kill this beetle with various pesticides, but the little sucker developed immunity to the poison. It nearly destroyed the entire Southern economy before it was done.

So the local cotton farmers, unable to bring the boll weevil to its figurative knees, realized they had the perfect climate for another crop: Peanuts. The region is now called "The Peanut Capital of the World."

Here's another example.

Decades ago, a 685-acre island in the Bahamas was populated with wild pigs. In 1980's Huntington Hartford purchased what was then called Hog Island, and began a major island make-over. It's now known as Paradise Island—one of the most attractive resorts in the Caribbean.

A few thoughts to ponder concerning these two stories: First, you never know what your current problem or major obstacle is worth. That's right! Your current problem could be an opportunity waiting to be discovered and unlocked. Often when we feel uneasy, we try to quickly brush off whatever is hindering us so we can once again feel comfortable. These two issues—a destroyed cotton crop, an uninhabitable island overrun by hogs—may have looked insurmountable at first, but they turned out to be goldmines for those who saw the opportunity in the midst of the problem.

Why Is Life Full of Problems?

Everyone was born to solve a problem. These problems are merely opportunities for you to discover your life purpose and existence on earth, which will eventually become your destiny. Problems are the gates to your significance. Problems link you to others. Problems are opportunities to reveal your unique abilities. Problems birth new relationships and friendships. Problems bring good people together during bad times. Problems provide your income and wealth. And if you remove problems from the earth, then you will destroy any sense of significance in humanity.

The problems that arrive in your life without your permission could be as little as a flat tire or as big as a divorce. And they are also unique and puzzling, which eventually sets you on a path to discovering your true assignment on earth, which you must first discover and then fulfill.

Most people miss out on some of the greatest blessings and breakthroughs in their life because they saw a problem as a problem and not as an opportunity. In the next section, you will learn about an amazing inventor who had several problems—but because of his proper attitude, he turned them into revolutionary opportunities for which the whole world is still grateful.

THE LIFE ATTITUDE OF THOMAS EDISON

Thomas Edison was an American inventor who is considered one of the greatest of all time But his humble beginnings may surprise you.

Edison did not learn to talk until he was almost four years old. One of his teachers said he was a poor and lazy student, since he was hyperactive and easily distracted. Edison was partly deaf, possibly due to a childhood attack of scarlet fever. He lost all of his hearing in his left ear and about eighty percent in his right ear. He only had about three months of formal public education before his mother began homeschooling him. But Edison, out of his curiosity to learn, read every book in the library starting with the last book on the bottom of the shelf.

When he was about twelve, he got a job selling newspapers, apples, and candy. At fifteen, he bought a small secondhand printing press and started producing the *Weekly Herald*, a newspaper he printed, edited, and sold. When he began to experiment with new innovations, Edison slept for an average of four hours a day, and often would work seventy-two hours straight, especially when completing an experiment.

In December 1914, Edison's plant burnt to the ground. When asked about it, however, Edison said, "We are rebuilding," and "we can make capital out of disaster."

In his lifetime, Edison made 1,093 inventions and held more than one thousand patents, which included the first light incandescent light bulb. He died at the ripe age of 84. Thomas Edison definitely had the instinct to see an opportunity within a problem.

Attitude Principles To Consider

•   Problems, challenges and obstacles are powerful sources for creativity and innovation. Learn how to embrace them.

•   Your problems and challenges are yours, and you are responsible for trying to discover a possible solution or breakthrough.

•   You always tolerate the things you are unwilling to change.

•   Don't expect any changes in your life while you are standing still and doing nothing.

•   Your problems will become your incubator for your attitude development.

•   Do not despise new challenges, since that is a sign of progress.

•   You were given a sophisticated brain to resolve problems, not to create more problems.

•   You will only be able to embrace greater challenges if you have the right mental attitude.

•   Your attitude will determine whether you see a problem in an opportunity or an opportunity in a problem.

Thomas Edison's attitude was to achieve what seemed to be impossible. Always remember that you were born to solve a specific problem (need) on this earth. But if you die without solving it, then you have robbed the next generation of something valuable.

So What Is Your Problem?

Allow me to quickly take you through the pages of history to point out some of the greatest inventions, ideas, businesses, companies, franchises and brands that were birthed during the *Great Depression*, which lasted from 1929 to 1940. And do take a close look at their most recent revenue and net worth.

- General Foods ($16.6 billion)
- Macy's ($25.7 billion)
- Sony Music ($4.9 billion)
- Walt Disney Pictures ($55.6 billion)
- GEICO ($25.5 billion)
- Krispy Kreme ($518 million)
- Metro-Goldwyn-Mayer ($1.4 billion)
- North American Van Lines ($1.9 billion)
- Ritz-Carlton ($3 billion
- Sheraton Hotels and Resorts ($6.1 billion)
- Allstate Insurance Co. ($36.5 billion)
- Duracell ($2 billion)
- Fisher-Price ($2.1 billion)
- Hostess Brands ($2.8 billion)
- Tyson Foods ($41.3 billion)
- Hasbro ($5 billion)
- Rubbermaid ($13.2 billion)
- Warner Bros. ($12.9 billion)
- Ryder ($6.5 billion)
- Hewlett Packard ($48.2 billion)
- Peterbilt ($4.7 billion)
- Steak 'n Shake ($806 million)

- Bridgestone Tires ($29. billion)
- Porsche ($25.3 billion)

- Advance Auto Parts ($9.7 billion)
- General Nutrition Centers ($2.6 billion)

- United Airlines ($36.5 billion)
- Dairy Queen ($1.8 billion)
- McDonald's ($24.6 billion)
- Walt Disney Studios ($92 billion)

Problems have always been and will remain with us. So will opportunities. Our attitude will determine if we are stuck in our past, confused in our present or fearful of the future. Make a decision today to stop looking at your problems as problems and to begin to see potential opportunities in the midst of these problems. Remember you were born to solve something specific on this earth, so make today the day when you set your attitude in the opportunity mode!

Attitude Questions To Consider

1. Do you currently have a problem or a possible opportunity?
2. Who should be most concerned about your problem?
3. Do you see the cup as half full or as half empty?
4. Are you part of the solution or part of the problem?

Chapter 4

<u>COMPLAINT OR CONSTRAINT?</u>

What Atmosphere Are You Creating?

Just keep in mind this one simple truth that nobody cares about your complaints. Even if someone patiently listens to you, at the end of it all, deep inside they still say to themselves *I don't care* as they smile back at you.

In April 2010 my lovely wife and I were traveling to Europe and got stranded at the Sheremetyevo International Airport in Moscow. A volcano erupted in Iceland, causing numerous flight cancellations that affected about ten million travelers. You can imagine the chaos at the airports! Many of our fellow passengers were aggravated and stressed out, and didn't bother hiding their anger and aggression, aimed mostly at the terminal clerks. As we waited patiently in line, we felt all the tension in the atmosphere as the passengers in front of us yelled and cursed at the clerks—and sometimes, the clerks returned the fire.

When our turn came, I was expecting to have all the clerk's pent-up fury unleashed on me. I chose to be polite and courteous—and surprisingly, the clerk treated me courteously and quickly served us with rescheduled tickets on the earliest flight that day. But as soon as we stepped away, the next passenger in line unleashed their anger and frustration, and in return the clerk fired back at them.

This became one of those teachable moments for me. The lesson was: I'm in control of my environment. I can either create a positive or negative atmosphere; I can cast more fuel or throw a bucket of water on the raging fire; and I can usher in the presence of peace or the presence of hellfire!

Our next individual arguably accomplished more behind prison bars then he did while in freedom.

THE LIFE ATTITUDE OF NELSON MANDELA

Nelson Mandela was imprisoned for twenty-seven years for his involvement in South Africa's anti-apartheid revolutionary movement. He became a lawyer to fight against the nation's system of racial segregation that favored whites. In 1961, he led a sabotage campaign against the government and in 1962, he was arrested for conspiring to overthrow the state.

As Mandela arrived on the island where he would be incarcerated for the next three decades, the white inmates shouted, *"This is the Island! Here you will die!"* But he showed the spirit of resistance that helped carry him through. During his years in prison he endured heavy labor, poor food, and inadequate winter clothing that left him shivering.

After Mandela was released from prison, he continued to fight against the apartheid system, which eventually ended in 1991, more than forty years after it began. Because of his passion for his country, he was elected as the country's first black head of state and the first elected in a fully representative democratic election; he served as president of South Africa from 1994 to 1999.

This rare opportunity led to some amazing things. He forgave everyone who participated in his imprisonments (including the harsh prison guards). "A good head and a good heart," Mandela often said, "are always a formidable combination."

Attitude Principles To Consider

•   The power of forgiveness is stronger than revenge.

•   Love like you've never been hurt before. This will be tough, but if Nelson Mandela could do it, so can you.

•   The ability to contain your frustration and anger is a sign of strength, not weakness.

•   You will never speak out against what you currently accept.

•   Every day we are faced with choices of what we accept and what we denounce.

•   Whoever lacks self-control over their own attitude is like a city broken down and without walls.

•   Complaining will only frustrate you and those around you, so STOP doing it.

•   There is no point in living a risk-free life and settling for less than what you are capable of.

•   Mandela once said, "There is no easy walk to freedom anywhere, and many of us will have to pass through the valley of the shadow of death again and again before we reach the mountaintop of our desires."

• When your mindset is wrong, your heart can never be right.

Nelson Mandela's enduring attitude was genuinely strong. His inner determination to fight for a powerful cause gave him the ability to contain his anger and frustration and to stay focused on the bigger issues at hand. He also learned that if you make too many enemies, this world becomes a dark place

About eighty thousand people and one hundred world leaders attended Nelson Mandela's funeral in 2013. That's more than Princess Diana's, Michael Jackson's and Pope John Paul II's combined, as reported by the International Business Times article. That speaks volumes about his impact; his legacy lives on.

Attitude Questions To Consider

1. How much have you achieved in life through your complaining?
2. Does your presence create a pleasant or sour atmosphere?
3. After a conversation, do people feel edified by you or drained out?
4. What type of atmosphere do you normally create in your life; in your home; in your workplace; amongst your friends?

Chapter 5

<u>MONDAY OR</u>
<u>MOANDAY?</u>

The Power of Dreaming Big

Everybody loves Mondays! Yeah right! After the short weekend is over, here comes *Moanday*, because many begin to moan as they once again get out of their comfortable beds and drive to work.

I once saw a billboard that said, "People who love Mondays," showing a woman with a big smile on her face—a minor encouragement for all the commuters moaning their way to work.

Here is a hypothetical thought: If you won the lottery, then Mondays would no longer be your Moandays, since you're financially set. But since that's not the case, you will be facing many more Mondays in your life. So suck it up and stop moaning!

Your mental attitude toward your current occupation will determine your outlook on future endeavors. And if you are not envisioning a brighter future, your weekly forecast will always seem cloudy and full of rain. As we move—without moaning—through the following pages, we will study ten billionaires and what made them so successful.

THE LIFE ATTITUDE OF TEN BILLIONAIRES

I specifically chose these ten billionaires because their humble beginnings did not hinder them from dreaming big. And even though their names are recognizable around the world, back in their day, they were just simple ordinary folks with big dreams.

Truett S. Cathy started first business adventure when he was just eight years old, selling soft drinks in his front yard. He later sold magazines and began a daily paper route at age twelve. In 1946, when he was twenty-five, he opened his first diner, called The Dwarf Grill, where he actually crafted a recipe for the first chicken sandwich. The little Dwarf Grill later became known as Chick-fil-A— which now has more than two thousand franchises nationwide and is worth an estimated $4.2 billion, despite every restaurant in the chain being closed on Sundays, which is considered the busiest eat-out day of the week.

Howard Schultz grew up in a government-subsidized housing complex for the poor. When he was seven years old, his father was injured at work. The family had no health insurance or worker's compensation, leaving them with no income. As an adult, Schultz began selling drip coffee machines; in early 1980's and a coffee shop in Seattle caught his attention when it ordered an unusually large number of them. The little coffee shop, called Starbucks, had four locations in the city. Intrigued, Schultz traveled to Seattle to meet the company's owners, and discovered their passion for coffee. It took Schultz about a year to persuade co-founder Gerald Baldwin to hire him as the director of marketing.

In 1987, Howard Schultz took over Starbucks as the company's CEO, and proceeded to grow the chain from the sixty operating at that time to more than twenty-seven thousand around the world today. Schultz's personal net worth is now approximately $3 billion.

One more important fact to consider about Schultz: As he was growing up, he witnessed how his father's employers often mistreated him. When he began his journey with Starbucks, he wanted to hold his employees in higher esteem. "I believe very strongly," he said, "that the success of our company has been achieved because of the relationship with our people." And according to Forbes list of *America's Best Employers*, in 2017 Starbucks ranked #179 for America's Best Employers; #26 Best employers for diversity, and #81 Worlds best employers.

Richard DeVos and ***Jay Van Andel*** had been friends and entrepreneurs since school days and business partners in various endeavors, including a hamburger stand, an air charter service, and a sailing business. In 1949, they were introduced to Nutrilite Products (multi-vitamins & supplements), and proceeded to build a network of more than five thousand distributors using multi-level marketing system. In 1959, they formed the American Way Association (Amway).

Their first product was soap. Over the decades, they expanded their network marketing business model into Australia, China, India, Europe, and Russia. In 1991, Rich DeVos bought the Orlando Magic NBA franchise; the team's home court is called the Amway Center.

Amway Corporation which started with two friends, has more than seventeen thousand employees worldwide;

holds eight hundred patents; includes more than 450 exclusive products; and has millions of independent entrepreneurial distributors in more than a hundred countries all over the world. The company generates more than $10 billion in sales per year. And according to Forbes, Rich Devos has a net worth of $5.4 billion and Jay Van Andel's net worth is $2.6 billion.

John Paul DeJoria is the man behind the hair-care empire John Paul Mitchell Systems and also Patron Tequila. But before he became a billionaire, he had his fair share of struggles: As a kid, he was sent to live in a foster home, and even spent some time in a gang. He was homeless twice, and sold encyclopedias, newspapers, and Christmas cards door-to-door just to make ends meet.

In 1980, he was fired from his job. With a $700 loan, he created John Paul Mitchell Systems and sold the shampoo door-to-door while living in his car. He later started Patron Tequila, and then more than a dozen other businesses. Today his net worth is around $3 billion.

"The biggest hurdle is rejection," he said once. "The difference between successful people and unsuccessful people is the successful people do all the things the unsuccessful people don't want to do."

Shahid Khan moved to the United States from Pakistan to study at the University of Illinois in 1967. His first job was washing dishes for $1.20 an hour, just to pay his expenses. In 1978, he started Bumper Works company, and in 1980 he bought Flex-N-Gate. He's now one of the richest people in the world who built one of the biggest automotive-parts suppliers in North America and one of the largest private companies in the U.S., which employs more than thirteen thousand people at fifty-two factories around the globe.

In 2011, he purchased the NFL's Jacksonville Jaguars for $700 million, becoming the first non-white team owner in NFL history. And in 2013 he purchased the London-based Fulham Football Club for $300 million. According to Forbes, Khan's net worth is around $7.1 billion.

Do Won Chang moved to U.S. from Korea in 1981 and worked as a janitor, as a gas station attendant, and in a coffee shop at the same time to make ends meet. He didn't go to college; in fact, he and his wife both barely finished high school.

While he was struggling to make ends meet, he felt the prices on clothes in retail stores were too high—saw it as an opportunity. He and his wife opened their first clothing store in 1984, and named it Forever 21. Today, Forever 21 is an international company with more than 600 stores and its net worth is $3.3 billion.

Leonardo Del Vecchio grew up in an orphanage. His father died five months before he was born, his mother gave him up to an orphanage because with four other children, she wasn't able to support him on her own. When he was fourteen, he went to work to support his impoverished adoptive family. He later picked up a fair amount of metal-working skill as an apprentice to a tool and die maker.

When he was twenty-three, Del Vecchio developed a fascination with eyeglasses and frames. He eventually opened his own molding shop, which expanded to become the world's largest maker of sunglasses and prescription eyewear, including the brands Ray-Ban and Oakley. Today, he employs more than seventy-five thousand workers across six thousand stores worldwide. His personal net worth is around $22.3 billion.

Sheldon Adelson was born to immigrants from Lithuania and Wales, and grew up sleeping on the floor of a Boston tenement house. As a child, he worked in a grocery store, a laundromat, a butcher shop, and sold newspapers. His first business breakthrough came at age twelve when he bought the corner newsstand where he'd been working.

Adelson dropped out of college and ran through a series of other jobs—candy vendor, mortgage broker, court stenographer. Eventually, he built a fortune selling newspaper ads, running vending machines, helping small businesses go public, developing condos, and hosting trade shows. He lost almost all his money when the recession hit between 2007 and 2009, but has earned much of it back. He is the founder, chairman, and chief executive officer of Las Vegas Sands Corporation, the largest casino company in the world, and has a net worth of $39 billion.

Larry Ellison was adopted when he was nine months old. He dropped out of college after his adoptive mother died, and held odd jobs for eight years.

In 1977, he co-founded Software Development Laboratories with an initial investment of $1,200. In 1982 the name was changed to Oracle Systems Corporation. Today, Oracle is one of the largest technology companies in the world, and the company has a net worth of $56.3 billion.

Attitude Principles To Consider

• Dream big, think big, and pursue your heart's passion.

• Truett S. Cathy once said, "Each person's destiny is not a matter of chance; it's a matter of choice. It's determined by what we say, what we do, and whom we trust."

• Howard Schultz once said, "I never wanted to be on any billionaires list. I never define myself by net worth. I always try to define myself by my values."

• Richard DeVos once said, "It is impossible to win the race unless you venture to run, impossible to win the victory unless you dare to battle."

• Jay Van Andel once said, "You can't predict the future, but you can follow your dreams."

• John Paul DeJoria once said, "I'll never retire. I like what I'm doing."

• Shahid Khan once said, "If you aren't learning, you are regressing, because more growth comes from failure than from success."

• Do Won Chang once said, "You can't go into business thinking that success will come to you in just one or two years."

• Sheldon Adelson once said, "An entrepreneur is born with the mentality to take risks, though there are several important characteristics: courage, faith in yourself, and above all, even when you fail, to learn from failure and get up and try again."

• Larry Ellison once said, "If you do everything that everyone else does in business, you're going to lose. The only way to really be ahead, is to be different."

The attitude of these ten billionaires should not make you jealous, but only hungrier for greater achievement and for re-adjusting your mindset from *Moanday* to Monday.

Here's a quick illustration. One day, two co-workers sat down for their lunch break. One of them pulled a bologna sandwich from his lunch box, looked at it and said, "Again, a bologna sandwich! This is now four days in a row I'm eating a stupid bologna sandwich. I'm already disgusted with these bologna sandwiches."

Surprised, his co-worker said, "Hey man, when you come home just tell your wife you don't want her to make you any more bologna sandwiches."
The first guy looked at him and responded, "My wife didn't make this sandwich—I did!"

It's easy to blame others for our stupid bologna-sandwich circumstances. If you have a bologna attitude, remember that you packed it yourself!

Attitude Questions To Consider

1. On Monday mornings, do you moan on the way to work?
2. Are you a dreamer or do you fantasize?

3. Do you look forward to Mondays or dread them?

4. On Monday mornings, do you wake up with a smile or a frown?

Chapter 6

<u>COMMERCIAL OR MOVIE?</u>

There Are No Shortcuts to Success

Wouldn't life be simple if we had a remote control for it, just like Adam Sandler did in the movie *Click*? Sure, we all dream of a sweet life, but the painful slap of reality is always hard for us to embrace!

So, what are commercials for? They're short, sweet and right to the point—and the point is for you to buy something! Since millions of dollars are continually invested into marketing a specific product or service, what makes you think you can take a shortcut toward your own success?

We often try to take a shortcut, like a commercial, only to be discouraged with the final results. Just because you saw a new movie trailer doesn't mean you know the whole storyline! Just because you read the first page of the book doesn't mean you know the full message! And sitting through one classroom lecture doesn't make you a knowledgeable expert on that subject!

The microwave mentality has given our society a commercial type of attitude. We don't want to invest our time or resources into something that requires work or effort. We just want to fast-forward to the end of the movie to find out what happens! But, there are no shortcuts in life, at least not the ones that will make you successful or influential.

If you ever have a chance to watch what goes on behind the scenes on any movie or TV show, you will be amazed how many time they may re-take the same scene over and over again just to make sure they get it right. And this doesn't include any unforeseen events, like a natural disaster or prop malfunction. Likewise, our attitude is not like a perfected thirty-second Super Bowl commercial; it requires work and discipline behind the scenes while no one is watching.

That said, we are definitely spoiled and even degraded by our fast-paced society, where everything can be done in an expedited way. We enjoy all these cultural or technological progressions, but we tend to neglect the fact that our attitude does not naturally or automatically upgrade itself within us the same way we might upgrade our smartphones! Our attitude is something that we need to continually work on, adjust and improve as we go through life.

Shortcuts might get you to your destination, but not without consequences. Reading one chapter from a book, will not give you the full story; going on one date, will not be enough to start a serious relationship; meeting someone for the first time, does not make you automatic friends; and having a one-time experience, does not qualify you as an expert!

History and life experience has proven that taking shortcuts or cutting corners or trying to get by through delusional luck, never made anyone genuinely successful.

This also applies to relationships, building a business, and so on, as our next featured individual will show.

THE LIFE ATTITUDE OF ARNOLD SCHWARZENEGGER

Here comes one of my childhood heroes. Let's grab a bag of popcorn and scroll through the life of Arnold Schwarzenegger—the Austrian-born professional bodybuilder, actor, producer, director, activist, philanthropist, businessman, investor, writer and politician.

Arnold's childhood was far from ideal. His father was an alcoholic police chief who also voluntarily joined the Nazi Party in 1938 and fought for Germany in World War II. When his father died of a stroke, Arnold was twenty-four years of age, and did not attend the funeral. In one interview, he stated that the reason was the abuse he suffered as a child at the hands of his father.

To get his focus off his dysfunctional family environment, Arnold started weight training when he was fifteen. He had so many posters of oiled-up bodybuilders covering the walls of his room that his parents at one point feared he might be gay.

In 1965, Arnold joined the Austrian Army for a mandatory time of service, and in that same year he won the Junior Mr. Europe contest. Two years later, he won the Mr. Universe contest for the first time—and at just twenty, he was the youngest ever to claim that title. There were times when Arnold was so hell-bent on working out as a youngster that he broke into local gyms when they were closed over the weekends.

Arnold moved to America in 1968, a dream he'd had since he was about ten years old. A few years later, he won his first Mr. Olympia title in New York, at age twenty-three. He went on to win that title seven more times over the course of his lengthy bodybuilding career.

Arnold had always dreamed of making it big in Hollywood. His first acting role was in 1970's *Hercules in New York*, playing the role of Hercules. In 1973, he made his second appearance as a deaf mute Mafia hit man in *The Long Goodbye*. In 1976 he started in his third movie, *Stay Hungry*, which earned him the 1977 Golden Globe for Best New Actor. Over his film career, he's had leading roles in more than thirty movies—but when he was just starting out, everyone told him he had no chance.

Schwarzenegger married Maria Shriver—an up-and-coming network news journalist and a niece of President John F. Kennedy—in 1986. In 2003, he was elected governor of California and served eight years in that capacity. Since he was already independently wealthy, he turned down the $175,000 annual salary and traveled in his own private jet on state business.

Now in his early 70s, Schwarzenegger is still making movies, and is not focused on retirement at all. His personal net worth is approximately $300 million. Schwarzenegger once said, "Strength does not come from winning. Your struggles develop your strengths. When you go through hardships and decide not to surrender, that is strength."

Attitude Principles To Consider

• Your mind is like a womb. Whatever seeds you sow into it will determine what you produce in your life.

• One big disability in your life is a bad attitude. So change your attitude in order to change your environment.

• If you accept your circumstance as your reality, you will begin to meditate on those circumstances, which will eventually give them more legal ground.

• Schwarzenegger once said, "Just remember, you can't climb the ladder of success with your hands in your pockets."

• "For me," Schwarzenegger said, "life is continuously being hungry. The meaning of life is not simply to exist, to survive, but to move ahead, to go up, to achieve, to conquer."

• Your dream is valuable, so start writing it down like a movie script and begin to organize a production team to make it happen.

• Your excuses for who you are—where you were born or how you were raised—will never justify failure.

• Dream big, but start with small clips. Eventually you will have a full movie.

• Your life is like a movie and you are the main actor. But how this movie ends depends on you.

Arnold Schwarzenegger's attitude to dream big and to achieve the impossible has definitely earned him a lifetime achievement award, because he did not make excuses for himself. You may choose to blame others for your lack, but that will fall on deaf ears. You may choose to point your figure at your parents, your upbringing, where you lived or what you had or didn't have, but all these things will eventually dissolve like vapor. Why? Because when you try to play the blame game and complain to others, then you begin to smell like skunk and no one will want to be around you.

Reality check! You are not the only one who had it rough and you are not the only one who had a truckful of problems dumped on you. So, let's take a positive life lesson from Arnold Schwarzenegger who did not take any shortcuts towards his incredible success.

Attitude Questions to Consider

1. Is your attitude like a microwave or a crockpot?
2. Are you trying to take shortcuts on the road to success?
3. Are you the director of your own movie or a continual critic?
4. Are you trying to build your success overnight?

Chapter 7
<u>MISTAKES OR LESSONS?</u>
Learn How to Fail Forward

Making mistakes is in our DNA. And due to our selfishness, pride, egotism and hardheadedness, it is only normal for us all to make mistakes. This has led to numerous books, articles, group meetings, and counseling sessions the world over.

Leadership expert John C. Maxwell dedicated a whole book to this issue, *Failing Forward* (Thomas Nelson, 2007). Maxwell points out that if you do fail, at least fail will the attitude of turning your mistakes into stepping stones for success.

Mistakes should never be seen as weakness, but only opportunities to learn and grow. Those who think they can avoid mistakes in life are delusional. The question is not whether you will make mistakes, but what you learn from them.

Sometimes mistakes open doors to remarkable innovations. As we journey forward, you will learn about eighteen people who invented revolutionary things by mistake.

EIGHTEEN THINGS THAT WERE INVENTED BY MISTAKE

1. Penicillin

Sir Alexander Fleming was a scientist who was experimenting with the influenza virus while searching for a "wonder drug" to cure diseases. At one point, he grew so frustrated with an experiment that he threw all his materials in the trash—but two weeks later, he noticed a culture plate he had discarded had begun to grow a strange mold. Interestingly, the influenza virus had stopped growing where the mold was present. The mold turned out to be penicillin., which eventually treated bacterial diseases.

2. Microwave Oven

Percy Spencer, an engineer with the Raytheon Corporation, was conducting research on how to detect German U-boats using radar during World War II. Spencer noticed that radiation from the machine he was using melted a chocolate bar in his pocket. He built a contraption using the rays from the radar detector—and just like that, the microwave oven was born. He experimented with popcorn; when it started to pop, he knew he had an innovative device on his hands.

3. The Slinky

Richard James was a mechanical engineer in the U.S. Navy, looking to create something that would stabilize and monitor machines on board ships. While working with tension springs in 1943, one of them accidentally fell to the ground and kept bouncing from place to place. James took it home to show the neighborhood kids, who loved it. For the next year, he tinkered with various types of wire and tensions, until he perfected the playful Slinky. As they say, "it's a wonderful toy."

4. Chocolate-Chip Cookies

Ruth Wakefield was the owner of the Toll House Inn, located in Whitman, Massachusetts. Back in 1937, while she was mixing a batch of cookies, Wakefield discovered she was out of melting baker's chocolate. As a substitute, she chopped a chocolate bar into bits and added them to the cookie dough. She expected the chips to melt as the cookies baked, but they didn't. Chocolate-chip cookies have been some of America's favorites ever since.

5. Potato Chips

One day in 1853, an angry customer sent his plate of potatoes back to New York chef George Crum, repeatedly asking for them to be crispier and thinner. Crum lost his temper, so he sliced the potatoes insanely thin, over-fried them until they were hard, and covered them with salt. To Crum's surprise, the customer loved them and wanted more! This was the birth of potato chips.

6. The Pacemaker

Electrical engineer Wilson Greatbatch was attempting to record electrical pulse sounds with a heart-rhythm recorder when he accidentally pulled the wrong resistor out of a box. When he re-assembled the device, instead of recording electrical pulses, it began emitting them. Greatbatch immediately realized he had just simulated a heartbeat, and this new invention could be used as a pacemaker. He spent roughly two years refining his device and was awarded a patent for world's first implantable pacemaker in 1962.

7. X-Rays

Wilhem Röntgen was an eccentric physicist who was interested in the properties of cathodic ray tubes. During an experiment, he noticed a piece of paper covered in barium platinocyanide began to glow from across the room. Not knowing what the rays were, he named it X-radiation, signifying its unknown nature. He also learned these rays could affect photographic plates. One day he took an X-ray photograph of his wife's hand that showed her bones and a ring. Röntgen was awarded the Nobel Prize for physics in 1901.

8. Saccharin

Constantine Fahlberg was a chemist at Johns Hopkins University in the late 1870s. While researching the way coal-tar derivatives interacted with each other, one of the compounds spilled on his hands. Since the chemical was nontoxic, he didn't bother to wash it off. But that evening while eating dinner, he noticed the bread tasted very sweet—and so did everything else he touched. The next day, Fahlberg isolated the compound that had spilled. He got a patent and began mass-producing his product, which we now use the world over as an artificial sweetener.

9. Fireworks

Two thousand years ago, an unknown cook in China accidentally spilled a mixture of saltpeter, sulfur and charcoal into a cooking fire, producing an interesting colorful flame. The cook noticed that if the mixture burned while enclosed in a hollow bamboo tube, it produced a tremendous explosion. This was the birth of the fireworks.

10. Corn Flakes

Dr. John Harvey Kellogg and his brother, Will Keith Kellogg, were searching for wholesome foods to feed their patients. As Seventh-Day Adventists, they followed a strict vegetarian diet. The brothers accidentally left a pot of boiled grain on the stove for several days, which made it go stale and moldy. Then they sent it through rollers, hoping to make long sheets of dough, but wound up with flakes instead. They toasted these flakes, which became a big hit with their patients. The brothers began experimenting with other grains and in 1906, Will created the Kellogg's company to sell corn flakes.

11. Post-It Notes

Spencer Silver, a researcher and chemist for 3M Laboratories, was trying (and failing) to make a heavy-duty adhesive. His compound stuck to objects, but could also be pulled off easily, without leaving a mark. It turned out to be useful for holding bookmarks in place and in 1974, the idea of removable notes was born. We now know his invention as Post-It Notes.

12. Plastics

Leo Baekeland was an industrial chemist who in 1907 accidentally created Bakelite, a plastic that is durable, moldable, non-conductive and heat-resistant. Earlier plastics had relied on organic material and were very expensive. The new thermosetting plastic was used for everything from phones to jewelry to clocks. It was also the first synthetic material to really stand on its own. Today, synthetic plastic is a common household item.

13. Stainless Steel

British metallurgist Harry Brearley was working to find an alloy strong enough to make gun barrels. Most gun barrels are grooved in a spiral pattern that causes the bullet to spin, but the friction between the barrel and the bullet causes wear; Brearley wanted to develop a steel alloy that would resist erosion. After much failure, his heap of steel scraps grew bigger and would usually rust. But, about a month into his experiment, he noticed one of the discarded barrels remained shiny. Upon further inspection, Brearley realized it wasn't only resistant to rust, but to almost all chemicals. He eventually called his new discovery "rustless steel." We know it now as "stainless steel," and see it in all kinds of appliances.

14. Popsicles

In 1905, eleven-year-old Frank Epperson mixed soda powder with water and left it on the back porch overnight with his stirring stick still in it. The temperature that night was extremely cold, and the next day he had a stick of frozen soda water to show his friends. Eighteen years later, Epperson remembered his frozen soda water mixture and began a business producing frozen drinks on a stick in seven fruit flavors. Today, popsicles are one of the world's favorite treats, especially on hot summer days.

15. Tea Bags

Thomas Sullivan was an American coffee and tea merchant who sent samples of his products to customers in packed cans. One day in 1903, he decided it would be less expensive to send the tea samples in small, hand-sewn silk bags, but his customers mistakenly thought the bags needed to be dropped into their cups for brewing purposes. To Sullivan's surprise, large amount of orders began pouring in, not for his tea, but for the bags. Why? Because these small bags had made brewing easier and more convenient. Today, more than half the tea consumed in American homes is made with tea bags.

16. Velcro

George de Mestral was a Swiss engineer. In 1941, he noticed that burdock burrs kept sticking to his clothes. He examined the burrs under a microscope, and discovered the hooks that made up the burrs would stick to any kind of loop. It took him about ten years of experimenting to develop a product made of two strips of nylon fabric; one contained thousands of small hooks and the other a corresponding number of small loops. When pressed together, they formed a strong bond.

17. Matches

John Walker, a British chemist, was stirring a pot of chemicals in 1826 when he noticed a dried lump had formed on the end of his mixing stick. Without thinking, he attempted to wipe the glob of chemicals off—but to his surprise, the glob burst into flame. Walker had an epiphany and began making tiny sticks about three inches long, covering one end with the chemical mixture. He sold the first strikable matches to a local bookstore, calling them "friction lights."

18. Ink-Jet Printers

An engineer working for Canon accidentally rested his hot iron on his pen. A few moments later, ink came squirting out. This principle later led to the creation of the inkjet printer, which has revolutionized the modern workplace.

Of course not every great innovation was discovered by a mistake, but these uncommon mistakes have definitely changed our way of life.

Attitude Principles To Consider

• Don't be afraid to make mistakes, since mistakes often give birth to new ideas.

• History teaches us that some of the greatest life lessons, inventions, ideas and cultural changes were discovered because of mistakes.

• Failure is not a sign of weakness, but only an opportunity to grow, to change, and to improve.

• If you are not willing to make mistakes, then don't expect to achieve greatness.

• Life is full of untapped opportunities, which are often discovered through mistakes.

• Those who never make mistakes are the ones who never tried anything new or different in life.

• Failure is the key to success, because each mistake can teach you something new.

• The only individual who never makes any mistakes is the one who never does anything.

• One of your best teachers is your last mistake.

These life-changing inventions only happened because these individuals were actually working on something and in the process they ended up with something they were not originally intending to accomplish. But we often quit when we are not able to accomplish something specific.

You cannot resurrect yesterday, and you are not guaranteed tomorrow, but you do have today. So put everything you've got into everything you do today. Remember, a mistake is not a conclusion, but an entry into another season.

Attitude Questions to Consider

1. Am I asking enough questions?

2. Do you feel like you need to have all the answers?

3. Are you focused on being right or doing right?

Chapter 8
PAIN OR PASSION?

Diamonds Are Formed Under Volcanic Pressure

There are many things in life that bring us pain, and fewer things that we are passionate about! For example, if you have children, are they a pain in the (*you fill in the blank*)? Or are they your passion? These questions can be applied to just about anyone in your life.

Yes, people who are especially close to us will eventually bring us pain. Spouses bring plenty of pain to each other. Children bring pain to their parents and vice versa. Employers bring pain to their employees. And of course, life brings on plenty of painful moments.

Does this mean we need to reject those who bring us pain? Absolutely not! The people and things we are most passionate about will cause us the most pain along the way. What? This sounds like an oxymoron.

While a woman is going through labor, she doesn't hate her unborn baby! Why? Because her inner, most passionate desire is to give birth to a new living being whom she will love, cherish, nurture, and admire. Even though she may be experiencing much pain and discomfort while in labor, she knows it's worth it because she is about to give birth to a living being.

And here is one more interesting truth to behold as it relates to precious diamonds, which the whole world admires. Diamonds are formed in the earth's mantle, where the temperature is about 2,000 degree Fahrenheit (1,050

Celsius). During deep source volcanic eruptions, and much pressure, they cause tears in the mantle and sent those pieces up to the surface. Because of the high pressure and temperature, carbon-containing fluids dissolved minerals and replaced them with diamonds.

With that said, pain is part of life. Pain in a sense creates an internal pressure, which makes us very uncomfortable, but if we are able to properly contain it then it will yield priceless results. Pain is also a necessity. Pain is a reminder that there is still room for growth. Pain helps you discover your inner purpose and passion. Don't run away from pain, but learn how to grow through it.

Which brings us to our next intriguing individual.

THE LIFE ATTITUDE OF RAY CHARLES

Ray Charles was a legendary musician. As a child he suffered from glaucoma, which made him completely blind by the age of seven. At Florida's Saint Augustine School for the Blind, he learned to read Braille and to play piano, clarinet and saxophone.

When he was fifteen, Charles' mother died. Two years later, his father also passed away. It seemed that suffering somehow produced in him a greater level of artistry. The texture of his voice, the way he mixed styles, and his emotional appeal produced a unique vocal artistry, which crossed language and racial barriers.

In the early stages of his career, Charles lived in poverty and often went without food for days. But with much persistence and passion, things began to shift: In 1960 Charles recorded "Georgia On My Mind" with ABC records, he became one of the first African American musicians to be given artistic control by a mainstream record company. No less than the legendary Frank Sinatra once said Charles was "the only true genius in show business."

But Charles had plenty of personal struggles. Recreational drug use led to an arrest year-long incarceration; he was also addicted to heroin for about sixteen years. He was married twice and fathered twelve children with ten different women.

Musically, however, he thrived. In 1981, he received a star on the Hollywood Walk of Fame, and was one of the first inductees in the Rock & Roll Hall of Fame at its inaugural ceremony in 1986. In 1993, he was awarded the National Medal of Arts; in 1998 he was awarded Sweden's Polar Music Prize.

Over his lifetime, Ray Charles recorded more than sixty albums, performed more than ten thousand concerts, and was highly admired by President Richard Nixon, as well as tens of thousands of other people. Charles, died in 2004 at the age of seventy-three, and left behind a legacy of joyful music.

Attitude Principles To Consider

- All you have to live up to is your best self. If you can do that, the rest of the things in life will take care of themselves.
- Don't go backward in life, you've already been there.
- Do not seek after fame or popularity—only greatness.

• You will never truly discover your passion until you experience pain.

• Pain is only a sign that lets you know that there is room for change; for growth; for maturity; and for discovering something new.

• Participation trophies are only given to those who were not willing to pay the ultimate price for success.

• Pain is not the enemy of your passion, but a coach and a mentor.

• Next time you encounter a successful person, ask them to show you their battle scars.

• Success will not be offered to you on a silver platter, but through sweat, tears, blood, failure and defeat.

• Rewards are not given to those who start the race, but to those who finish it.

Ray Charles' attitude for life and for success qualifies him to be admired and highly respected, even though he had his fair share of downfalls. Just like Helen Keller, Ray never used his disability as an excuse for doing less, and was not looking for a handout! And we should not get distracted by the painful moments or seasons of our life, but stay focused on our passion and dreams. "Sometimes my dreams are so deep," Charles said, "that I dream that I'm dreaming."

Even though we can experience pain in the night, our passion gives us the opportunity to look forward to the joy that will come in the morning. Do not build upon the foundation of pain, but build on the foundation of passion!

Attitude Questions to Consider

1. Do you focus on the power of your future or on the pain of your past?

2. Do you use pain as an opportunity to move forward or as an excuse to quit?

3. Are you moved by passion or by position?

4. Are you passionate or passive?

Chapter 9

CAT OR LION?

Discover Your Purpose in Life

Recently, I have been intrigued by lions and why they are considered the king of the jungle. After watching a handful of documentary videos, I've come to a conclusion: The lion may be king of the jungle, but the house cat is the king of the couch!

I was never an enthusiastic cat fan, but my youngest daughter kept begging me and my wife to get her one. Eventually, we adopted some else's cat, named Princess. Great looking and potty trained!

Just when I thought that I was getting attached to Princess, I realized something: A house cat is the laziest, most purposeless animal you can have as a pet. (Please, cat lovers—don't send me any nasty letters or negative book reviews on Amazon. Don't get me wrong, she is a cute fur ball, but my entrepreneurial and visionary characteristics do not align with the behavior characteristics of a cat. I guess we just have a love-hate relationship for now.)

As I have mentioned, I'm a visionary person with great ambitions and an entrepreneurial attitude; Princess is a lazy couch potato who naps most of the day and meows every time she is hungry or wants to go outside. That said, I think God has a real sense of humor in allowing this cat to be dropped off at our doorstep during one of the most critical, transitional seasons of my life. Why, so I can stay focused on my dreams and things that I'm passionate about without procrastinating.

Lions, on the other hand, hunt for their own food and defend themselves and their fellow pride members. The lion takes risks; it can easily attack and overpower animals twice its size. It has the patience to lie in wait and ambush its prey.

Our attitude reflects on our behavior patterns and on our daily habits. During my leisure time, do I just sit back and binge on a full season of my favorite TV series or surf through social media for hours? Or do I take advantage of these much-needed moments to pursue my dreams, my purpose, and my passion? There's a lot we can learn about this from our next featured individual.

THE LIFE ATTITUDE OF OPRAH WINFREY

Oprah Winfrey was raised on a farm by her grandmother, but later in life moved in with her mother, stepsister and step brother in an inner-city ghetto. During that time, she suffered abuse and was even raped by her uncle, a cousin, and a family friend. When she was thirteen, she ran away from home and barely escaped being sent to a juvenile detention center. When she was fourteen was raped again and gave birth to a premature boy, who died soon afterward.

In high school, Winfrey was an honors student, was voted Most Popular Girl, and joined the school speech team. At seventeen, she won the Miss Black Tennessee beauty pageant and the Miss Fire Prevention title. After high school, she attended Tennessee State University. During her sophomore year, she become the youngest and first African-American reporter for WTVF-TV in Nashville. She did poorly as a reporter, and when she was twenty-two, she was fired from the news division.

But Winfrey didn't let that stop her from pursuing her broadcasting dreams. In 1984, she becomes the anchor of a local television program called *A.M. Chicago.* Soon afterward, it was renamed *The Oprah Winfrey Show* and broadcast nationally. During its run from 1985 to 2011, it became the highest-rated talk show in history, earning Winfrey sixteen Daytime Emmy Awards.

In 1985, Oprah formed her own company, Harpo Productions; in 1988 she was named broadcaster of the year by the International Television and Radio Society. In 1996, she launched Oprah's Book Club; the books she recommended sold millions of additional copies. In 2002, she launched *O, the Oprah Magazine*—the most successful start-up ever in the magazine industry.

In 2004, Winfrey was listed as the world's only black billionaire and was named by *Time* as one of the one hundred most influential people of the twentieth century. Winfrey's current net worth is more than $3 billion.

Not bad for a runaway girl who was raped as a teen. She definitely has the heart of a lion!

What does that mean? Here are a few surprising facts: The lion is not the strongest. The lion is not the fastest. The lion is not the smartest. And the lion is not the largest or the tallest. But he is considered the king of the jungle because of his attitude.

Oprah decided not to be a house cat who was looking for a handout or for someone to pity her. She understood her future was in her own hands, and her attitude to achieve what the seemingly impossible has been leading her to ever-greater heights.

Attitude Principles To Consider

• You need to be a fighter! Not a fighter with people, but a fighter within your mind by continually disciplining yourself to overcome every obstacle.

• Don't allow the color of your skin, your rough childhood, or anything else to become an obstacle that keeps you from fulfilling your purpose and heart's desire.

• Life will come crashing hard on you, but what you do after that will determine your future.

• It's possible for you to achieve greatness without blaming everyone and everything around you for the bad things that happen.

• Excuses and blame has never made anyone influential or won them the admiration of millions around the whole world.

• "When you undervalue what you do," Winfrey once said, "the world will undervalue who you are."

• Throughout your life, you will come across many challenging situations, but your attitude will determine your next steps.

• You were born for a purpose in order to fulfill a purpose. So don't live your life in futility.

• Success is always possible for those who refuse to stop fighting.

• When you discover your purpose, you will begin to have a clear idea for your existence.

Winfrey once summed these ideas up by saying, "Turn your wounds into wisdom." With that said, let us begin to re-adjust our couch attitude and turn it into an adventurous jungle, as we roam through life like the king (queen) of the jungle!

Attitude Questions to Consider

1. Have you discovered your purpose?

2. Are you sitting around like a cat waiting for a handout, or are pursuing your dreams and ambitions like a lion?

3. Do you want to live a purposeful or a purposeless life?

Chapter 10

<u>CONTRACT OR COMMITMENT?</u>

Are You Average or Rare?

Most often the terms *contracts* and *commitments* have to do with business or marriage. But I would like to expand to include your thinking and behavior patterns.

Commitment has to do with honesty and integrity, while a contract could be easily broken. A committed individual does not compromise, but often people will embrace compromise in order to get a contract. Compromise in itself has many variations, but is often is a grey area where you will be tested.

When you have an attitude of commitment, then you tend to discipline yourself as best you can. But if you have the attitude that a contract can easily be broken or changed, you're not very disciplined and could be easily swayed away in any direction.

Our world is saturated with average individuals. Our workplaces are full of average employees. Many of our modern leaders are only operating in the average mode, and sadly we are even grooming an average generation by saying anything goes. For example, why in the world do car manufacturers design vehicles with speedometers that go up to 150 mph, while most average roads in USA have a speed limit of 65 mph?

When we ask children what they want to be when they grow up, they say things like, "I want to be a billionaire," or "I want to be an astronaut," or "I want to become the president," or "I want to create a new invention that will revolutionize the whole world." As parents and teachers, we think those dreams are great—but tragically, in reality, parents tend to cool off their children's dreams, adults ignore them, and our modern academia is not structured to nurture and develop them. Instead, we encourage our children to get an education (which is average in this country, and less than average compared to what it was a hundred years ago and to others in the world now), so they can get a secure (average) job. I share more about this in Chapter 18. I'm not bashing academia or teachers, but the fact is that our educational concepts and practices have drastically changed over the years.

Are we raising a rare generation or an average generation? Is our academia structured to groom average or rare individuals? Is our culture structured in a way to welcome average individuals who will exist in our society or rare individuals who will transform it? Remember, diamonds are rare and that is why they are so expensive. Let's take a quick look at a well-known coach whose life of commitment has made him a legend. Why? Because he chose to become rare.

THE LIFE ATTITUDE OF JOHN WOODEN

John Wooden was raised on a farm in Indiana, with no electricity. He worked hard, but also found time for fun by playing basketball in a barn with his three brothers. Wooden became a star basketball player at Martinsville

High School, leading the team to the Indiana State championship in 1927. He was a three-time high school all-state selection.

Wooden went on to earn three consecutive All-America selections as a guard at Purdue University and was named team captain as a junior. After winning the College Basketball Player of the Year Award, his team became national champions in 1932. He graduated with honors, then spent several years playing professionally with the Indiana Kautskys (later the Indianapolis Jets), while teaching and coaching high school teams.

His first coaching job was at Dayton High in Kentucky; in his first year, the team went 6-11, which was his only losing record as a coach. By the end of his 11-year high school coaching career, his record was 218-42. In 1946, Wooden was hired at Indiana Teachers College (now Indiana State University) as an athletic director, baseball and a basketball coach for two seasons before moving to the University of California-Los Angeles, where he spent the next twenty-seven years.

Wooden's top salary coaching at UCLA was $35,000. At one point, he turned down an offer to coach the Los Angeles Lakers, at a salary ten times higher; he was committed to his college team. Under his leadership, the Bruins won nineteen conference championships, had four 30-0 seasons, and a record winning streak of 88. Wooden gained long-lasting fame with UCLA by winning 664 games in twenty-seven seasons, and brought home ten NCAA Division I titles during his last twelve seasons.

Wooden was inducted into the Basketball Hall of Fame both as a player (class of 1961) and as a coach

(1973). He was the first person ever enshrined in both categories. In 1972, he was honored as Sports Illustrated's Sportsman of the Year. And since 1977, college basketball's most prestigious postseason award has been called the John R. Wooden Award.

In 1999, ESPN named Wooden "Coach of the 20th Century" and in 2003, he received the Presidential Medal of Freedom, the nation's highest civilian honor. Throughout his life, Wooden exemplified passion as a coach and mentor.

Attitude Principles To Consider

- Always be teachable. Then you will be able to effectively teach others.
- Your character is more important than your reputation or accomplishments.
- The younger generation needs more authentic role models, not more critics.
- If you are true to yourself, you will eventually be honest with everyone else.
- When you discipline yourself daily, others won't need to.
- Dream big and don't allow your dreams to die.
- Don't try to be somebody else. Be original, which make you rare and valuable.
- If you are not making mistakes, then you're not doing anything.
- Don't allow criticism or praise to grab hold of you; it will become your weakness.

• John Wooden once said, "Be more concerned with your character than your reputation, because your character is what you really are, while your reputation is merely what others think you are."

John Wooden's attitude as a coach made him stand out from the crowd. "In the end, it's about the teaching, and what I always loved about coaching was the practices," Wooden said once. "Not the games, not the tournaments, not the alumni stuff. But teaching the players during practice was what coaching was all about to me."

In order to succeed greatly, you must be willing to fail greatly. Great success comes with a heavy price tag; those who are not willing to pay it will always be average.

Attitude Questions to Consider

1. How committed are you to what you are doing?
2. Are you content where you are right now in your life?
3. Is your purpose under a contract or under a commitment?
4. What kind of legacy do you want to leave when you die?

Chapter 11
<u>DIVISION OR MULTIPLICATION?</u>
Adding Value to Others

Have you ever asked a chubby woman when she was due, and it turned out she wasn't even pregnant? Not only did she probably skewer you with a look, but you walked away feeling like a total jerk who had made this woman feel less positive about herself than before she ran into you. Or maybe you've been on the receiving end of a demeaning or cutting remark that someone else thought was "just a joke."

The attitude of adding value to others begins with words and is followed by actions. Unfortunately, we often don't pay attention to our words. When you don't have anything of value to talk about, then you go into your "nothing box" (which every person has), and pull out of it empty words that add no value to the conversation.

It's no surprise that we're constantly being bombarded with divisive words, useless conversations, negative environments, and frustrated individuals. We can't always avoid them or tune them out, but we should never become victims of them.

Our next featured individual had a physical disability her whole life, but used it not only to her own advantage, but also to add value to others!

THE LIFE ATTITUDE OF HELEN KELLER

Helen Adams Keller was an American author, political activist and a lecturer. She was the first deaf-blind person to earn a bachelor of arts degree. She was originally born with both her sight and hearing, but when she was about eighteen months old, she became very ill and lost both.

Around age six, Helen was introduced to Anne Sullivan, who became her personal teacher, and their relationship lasted for forty-nine years. The first word Keller learned was "water," and by the end of that day she had learned thirty others.

By the time she was sixteen, Keller could not only read Braille, use the typewriter and write, but could speak fluently enough to attend college. She graduated from Radcliffe College *cum laude* in 1904. She was the first deaf-blind person to write a book, and published fourteen of them during her life.

Keller was a major globetrotter who traveled to thirty-nine countries, meeting with presidents, prime ministers, and other government leaders to advocate for educating blind, deaf, and disabled people. She also visited veteran's hospitals during World War II to encourage those who lost their sight in battle injuries.

Keller's passion for serving others earned her a nomination for the 1953 Nobel Peace Prize. She met every U.S. president in office between 1988-1964. "The only thing worse than being blind," she once said, "is having sight but no vision."

Keller lived to the ripe age of 87 and died in her sleep in 1968. In 1999, *Time* magazine named her one of the most important people of the 20th century, on a list that included Mahatma Gandhi, Franklin D. Roosevelt, and Albert Einstein. In 2003, the U.S. Treasury released a new quarter with Helen Keller's face on it and the phrase "Spirit of Courage."

Wow, Helen Keller was truly an exceptional individual who confronted her physical infirmities with a positive attitude. And by doing so, she accomplished more in her life than millions of perfectly healthy individuals combined. Keller did not become an influential or highly respected person because of her blindness and deafness, but because of her attitude for making a difference in the world.

No ordinary individual ever becomes famous, admirable, influential, or highly honored by doing nothing! Whether you are rich or poor, black or white, disabled or in perfect health, highly educated or a high school dropout, you can discover your inner purpose and potential. Keller knew who she was, and that allowed her to bring a positive multiplication effect into the world.

Attitude Principles To Consider

- Don't focus on your weaknesses or on your outward imperfections, but on your inner identity and the value you can add to others.
- Your character cannot be developed comfort, but only through trials and suffering.

- Life is either a great adventure or nothing, so you need to decide to live your life to the fullest.
- Optimism gives you the faith to achieve great things.
- Your life can be a great adventure or a stumbling block to others. The choice is up to you.
- Since the world is already full of pain and suffering, don't become another contributor.
- Don't be just a consumer in life, but a giver and a multiplier of hope and happiness.
- The hope for this world lies within you.
- Allow the world to discover who you are.

Helen Keller's productive and influential attitude of multiplication should take away your every excuse. Likewise, we should also possess an attitude that brings multiplication and growth into the lives of those who surround us on a daily basis.

Attitude Questions to Consider

1. Are you passing the baton or holding onto it?

2. Are you a team player or just a player on the team?

3. Are you "people" focused or are you "me" focused?

4. Is your attitude one of division or multiplication?

Chapter 12

<u>REVENGE OR RELEASE?</u>

Forgive Like You've Never Been Hurt

We all have been guilty of doing something bad in our lives—even the cutest, most cuddly-looking one-year-old among us! Even though our wrongdoings will vary, we cannot ignore the fact that whether big or small, they hurt others. Then we are faced with a choice: What we are willing to do to resolve the matter?

Of course, this goes both ways; at times, we fall prey to someone else's evil intentions. But again, our heart attitude determines the route you take to receive emotional, mental, spiritual, or psychological release.

This is reality: In life, you will be offended! You will be lied to! You will be cheated out of something! You will be betrayed! You will be rejected! You will be used! You will be taken advantage of! And yes, your heart will be broken at some point! *Yeah, Stan, I thought this was supposed to be one of those uplifting motivational books!* It is, and I just gave you an opportunity to look into the mirror of reality!

Humans can be selfish and self-centered, and we are hardwired with a natural instinct to survive. So when others do us wrong, we're going to feel it. No matter what hellish situation you might have faced or experienced in your life, let's first take a look at the life of an individual who has a few words of advice for us all.

THE LIFE ATTITUDE OF LOUIS ZAMPERINI

Louis Zamperini truly had an amazing story. He was a track star who ran in the 1936 Berlin Olympics. He received a compliment from Hitler as he shook his hand. He enlisted in the U.S. Air Corps and in 1943, while on a rescue mission, his plane crashed in the Pacific Ocean, killing eight of the ten other crew members aboard. The three survivors were stranded at sea for forty-seven days, drifting on a life raft in shark-infested waters for two thousand miles, with only a few bottles of water and six chocolate bars between them.

They survived. But when they finally made it to an island, they immediately found it was occupied by the Japanese Navy. They were taken captive, held for six weeks, and then shipped to the Japanese mainland where they were confined to three different interrogation centers and POW camps. During his two years as a Japanese POW, he endured disease, starvation and daily beatings from the guards, who pummeled him with clubs, belts, and fists.

After the Japanese surrendered to Allied forces, Zamperini was freed. But the trauma he suffered gave him nightmares and flashbacks. He developed a drinking problem and his wife nearly left him. But after attending a Billy Graham evangelistic crusade, he found faith in God—and was able to find peace. And he forgave the Japanese prison camp guards who had made his life a literal hell for so long.

In 1950, Zamperini returned to Tokyo, where he met with his former guards—who were serving prison sentences for war crimes—and told them he forgave them. In 1998, he went back to Japan to carry the Olympic torch for the winter games in Nagano; the route took him right past the prison where he'd suffered so much.

Having endured so much over his life, Louis died at the ripe old age of 97. "The one who forgives never brings up the past to that person's face," Zamperini said once. "When you forgive, it's like it never happened. True forgiveness is complete and total." Louis Zamperini was just an ordinary man, but his attitude made him into an extraordinary person.

Attitude Principles To Consider

•   Forgiveness is a choice; the choice is always yours to make.

•   Reach deep within yourself to see if you are willing to make the necessary sacrifices.

•   Don't give up and don't give in.

•   Always be willing to fight the good fight, but also be willing to forgive those who hurt you.

•   When you have hatred toward someone, you automatically imprison yourself.

•   One of the hardest things in life is to forgive, but to hate is self-destructive.

•   Be resilient; be brave; be forgiving. Revenge is a sign of weakness.

•   Our prisons and jails are full of individuals who were not able to release and forgive those who hurt (victimized) them.

Louis Zamperini's willingness to release his enemies through forgiveness should not be left as a deed in the pages of our history, but made into a powerful life principle that we all need to seriously consider, since most of what we struggle to forgive doesn't rise to the level of torment he suffered.

Attitude Questions to Consider

1. When was the last time you forgave someone?

2. Are you storing offense in your heart or building up forgiveness?

3. Last time you avenged yourself, how did that work out for you?

4. Are you willing to persevere or just thrown in the towel of surrender?

Chapter 13

FEAR OR FAITH?

Success Requires Taking Risks

There is a reason why this particular chapter is under the lucky number thirteen: For me, it represents many blessings, since the love of my life was born on September 13.

Anyway, *fear* is a negative emotion which is often triggered by a lack of identity, doubt, and insecurity. It is the opposite of faith, which is a positive mental attitude that allows you to expect the impossible to become possible and for the unseen to become a reality.

Anxiety causes health problems, family problems, and social problems. Why? Because you are continually bombarding your subconscious with thoughts of fear, which activate feelings of insecurity.

Are you a worrier or a warrior? Are you looking for safety and security or a thrilling adventure? Of course, we all seek exciting new opportunities in life, but a void of faith will always be filled with fear. Remember, how *long* you live is not as important as *how* you live. Those who refuse to take risks also seem to do most of the complaining in our society.

Fear and faith will never be able to coexist, but both of them are continually vying for your attention! Our next individual exemplified faith when she could have chosen fear, many times over.

THE LIFE ATTITUDE OF MARY KAY ASH

Mary Kay Ash became as a salesperson for Stanley Home Products in 1939, hosting parties to encourage people to buy household items. She was so good that another company hired her away in 1952. Ash spent a little more than a decade there—but after repeatedly watching the men she trained get promoted over her for higher salaries, she finally quit in protest.

So at the age of forty-five, Ash set out to create her own business. She started with an investment of $5,000, purchasing the formulas for skin lotions from a tanner who created them. Ash eventually opened a small store in Dallas.

As she launched her own cosmetics company, she began using incentive programs for her employees, giving them a chance to benefit from their achievements. Ash's marketing and people skills soon led her company to enormous success: It turned a profit in its first year with sales of nearly $1 million.

Ash lived by The Golden Rule: Treat others as you want to be treated. She also operated by the principle that God is first, family second and career third. She was known for her love of the color pink, which was visible in her products and the Cadillac's she gave to top-earning consultants each year. Ash traveled the world to empower people to change their lives for the better.

In 1996, she established the Mary Kay Charitable Foundation, which supports cancer research and efforts to end domestic violence. Today, more than three million people worldwide are Mary Kay Independent Beauty

Consultants. More than thirty-nine thousand women across the world are Independent Sales Directors. And more than six hundred women worldwide have become Independent National Sales Directors, the highest status within the sales force. Today the company has a net worth of $4 billion.

Mary Kay Ash received many honors over her life:

- Horatio Alger Distinguished American Citizen Award (1978)
- Pathfinder Award, National Association of Women Business Owners (1995)
- National Business Hall of Fame (1996)
- "Most Outstanding Woman in Business in the 20th Century," Lifetime Television (1999)
- Baylor University's "Greatest Female Entrepreneur in American History" (2003)
- PBS and the Wharton School of Business's "25 Most Influential Business Leaders of the Last 25 Years" (2004)
- "100 Greatest Women of 100 Years," YWCA of Metropolitan Dallas (2008)

Mary Kay Ash left a lasting imprint in the hearts and lives of millions of women, including those who are not part of her current company.

Attitude Principles To Consider

- Fear attracts obstacles, but faith attracts opportunities.

- Walk by faith and not by what your limited sight allows you to see.
- Your faith should never be contingent on or limited by others; you are in control of your life and your destiny.
- Faith gives you the ability to see the invisible and to believe for the impossible.
- One of the best ways for you to stir up your inner faith is to tune out the voices of limitation and tune into what your heart is telling you.
- Build your confidence so you can destroy your fears.
- Faith is the key to unlocking doors of opportunity; fear is a lock that will conceal doors of opportunity.
- Never give up trying to build your dream, even if others can't see it.
- You need to be faithful in small things, since your strength lies in them.
- Virtually nothing is impossible, if you just put your mind to it and maintain a positive mental attitude.

Mary Kay Ash's attitude made her one of the most successful female entrepreneurs of the last century, because she was willing to get out of her comfort zone. Not to take any risks, is a risk in itself! Why? Because risks carry a two-sided character and function where on one side it could be your best friend or your worst enemy.

Let us learn how to tune out the inner loud voices of fear by re-adjusting our attitude, so we can begin to hear the small still voice, which gives faith and encourages us to move forward.

Attitude Questions to Consider

1. Are you currently full of fear of faith?

2. When was the last time fear opened the doors of opportunity for you?

3. Do you have a vision or an excuse?

Chapter 14
<u>GREED OR NEED?</u>
The World is Much Bigger Than You

Greed has the ability to wear you out physically, emotionally, mentally, and spiritually. Money, prosperity, and success in business are positive things, but could also come with a hefty price tag.

Let's do an honest evaluation of the word *greed* and how it applies to specific areas of life. Yes, greed can apply to just about anything, but the truth is that greed and money go together like a husband and wife. So, let's do a reality check with this question: When I say the word *greed*, what is the first thing that comes to your mind?

Here's one example of greed—and stinginess: "I won $4 million on the lottery this weekend so I decided to donate a quarter of it to charity. Now I have $3,999,999.75."

You can also be greedy with your time, your talents or skills, or your much-needed life experience! Greed is not limited to monetary things, but anything you could do to benefit your fellow man, but choose not to.

Our next two generous individuals chose to benefit their fellow men through generosity, because they both understood that the world is much bigger than who they are, and they wanted to become an asset and not a liability.

THE LIFE ATTITUDE OF REV. EDGAR J. HELMS AND WILLIAM BOOTH

Goodwill

Goodwill was founded in 1902 in Boston by the Rev. Edgar J. Helms, a Methodist minister and early social innovator. Helms collected used household goods and clothing in wealthier areas of the city, then trained and hired the poor to mend them. The goods were then resold or given to the poor. The system worked, and the Goodwill philosophy of "a hand up, not a hand out" was born.

Helms's vision set an early course for what today is a $5 billion nonprofit organization. Helms described Goodwill Industries as an "industrial program as well as a social service enterprise ... a provider of employment, training and rehabilitation for people of limited employability, and a source of temporary assistance for individuals whose resources were depleted."

According to Goodwill's success stories, they claim that approximately every 23 seconds of every business day, a person served by Goodwill earns a good job. In 2016, more than 313,000 people used Goodwill services to help them connect to jobs in their communities. Every year, keeps more than three billion pounds of used clothing and household goods out of landfills by reselling them through its 2,800 shop Goodwill has a strong presence in the United States, Canada and serves in around 17 other countries.

The Salvation Army

The Salvation Army was founded in 1865 by street evangelist William Booth and his wife, Catherine. They withdrew from the church to train evangelists throughout England where they mainly focused on thieves, prostitutes, gamblers, and drunkards. Their ministry was first called The Christian Mission; when Booth noticed in his annual report the statement, "The Christian Mission is a volunteer army," he officially changed it to The Salvation Army.

The annual Red Kettle Christmas fundraising campaign started in 1891 when a Salvation Army captain in San Francisco set up a crab pot and began collecting money for the poor. Since then, the Red Kettle Campaign has become one of the longest-running fundraising efforts in the world, including Asia, Europe, and South America. According to the Salvation Army's 2017 annual report, it raised $2 billion through the Red Kettle campaign that year.

The money raised though The Salvation Army for over a course of a century, has definitely been a remarkable achievement, since they were able to create a giving atmosphere and stir the hearts of millions of individuals to sow into the lives of the needy and the poor.

Through the revenue from its thrift stores, the Salvation Army is able to provide free rehabilitation services for alcohol and drug addicts. Since 1885, the group has been striving to restore families who've lost contact with each other, helping thousands every year.

In 2001, the Salvation Army began dispensing food and drinks near Ground Zero less than an hour after the terrorist attacks on the World Trade Center in New York City. In about nine months of service there, forty thousand Salvation Army volunteers, officers, and staff assisted more than four million people with meals, social services, and pastoral counseling.

The Salvation Army currently operates in 128 countries across the globe and provides services in 175 different languages with the mission of bringing salvation to the poor, the hungry, and the destitute by meeting their physical and spiritual needs. It has more than 1.5 million members assisting approximately twenty-five million Americans annually.

Attitude Principles To Consider

• Edgar J. Helms once said, "Friends of Goodwill, be dissatisfied with your work until every handicapped and unfortunate person in your community has an opportunity to develop to his fullest usefulness and enjoy a maximum of abundant living."

• William Booth once said, "If you want to change the future, then you are going to have to trouble the present."

• It is impossible to warm the hearts of the needy if we are not willing to serve them.

• Servanthood is a sacrifice of your personal time and finances.

• Greed will blind you to the needs of others and make your ears deaf to those who are hurting.

• Those who are greedy for more gain will expose themselves to various types of trouble and headaches.

• Seeing a need only takes your eyes, but to fulfill that need requires a decision of your heart.

• Greed is not always a monetary issue, but often a heart issue.

The Salvation Army's and Goodwill's philosophy and business models are definitely exceptional. Both William Booth and Edgar J. Helms dreamed of reaching out to the poor and ill-equipped to give them an opportunity to make a living. Both understood a deeper need and decided to create an unconventional business model, which has been working effectively for decades.

Attitude Questions to Consider

1. Are you a giver or a taker?
2. Is your heart driven by greed or by need?
3. Are you money-focused or vision-focused?
4. Are you controlling your finances or are they controlling you?

Chapter 15

<u>BITTER OR BETTER?</u>

Giving Hope to The Hopeless

Ⅰn Chapter 12, we focused on forgiving your enemies and oppressors, but here I want to draw your attention on how you can turn your tears into hope; how to turn your ashes into beauty; how you can exchange mourning for joy; and how you can turn a raging storm into a warm sunny day.

Tragedy and unexpected trials of life never ask permission to come crashing in! But when they do, don't get bitter. Trying to find hope in your fiery circumstances will result in your betterment and quick recovery.

To be frank, this book stems from things I learned during unpleasant season's of my life. Choosing to focus on the bright side allowed me to overcome my negative circumstances. During those dreadful season's of my life, my wife and I were often humbled when we heard about other people's tragedies, which were far worse than ours. That always helped us adjust our attitudes, and kept us thankful for the good things we had.

Over the years, I've often asked myself, *How much better off will this world be because of who I am and what value I can add to others?* Our next individual did the same—turning her bitter situation into a hopeful mission.

THE LIFE ATTITUDE OF CANDACE LIGHTNER

Candace Lightner founded Mothers Against Drunk Driving (MADD) after her thirteen-year-old daughter, Cari, was killed by a drunk driver in 1980. MADD is a nonprofit organization in the United States and Canada that seeks to stop drunk driving; prevent underage drinking; support those affected by drunk driving; and strive for stricter impaired-driving policies, whether that impairment is caused by alcohol or any other drug.

Four days after Cari's death, Lightner started a grassroots organization to advocate for stiffer penalties for drunk driving. She eventually quit her job and used her personal savings to fund MADD. Lightner proved to be a tireless fighter, and visited California Gov. Jerry Brown's office on a daily basis until he launched a state commission on drunk driving.

In 1984, President Ronald Reagan appointed her to the National Commission on Drunk Driving. Through MADD, Lightner helped get more than four hundred new drunk-driving laws passed in individual states and also federally, including raising the legal drinking age to twenty-one.

Since its founding, MADD has saved 330,000 lives. It gained two million members in its first three years of operation, and currently has four hundred chapters across the globe. "The road through grief is a rocky one," Lightner once said. "Traveling along it requires courage, patience, wisdom, and hope."

Candace Lightner was able to turn her bitterness into betterment, and created a national movement in the process.

Attitude Principles To Consider

•   Bitterness can dry up your spirit and divert you from your destiny.

•   Pain can help you discover hidden gems of passion and purpose.

•   Bad things will happen, so the best preparation is a positive attitude.

•   Your attitude is a little thing that could make a big difference in your life and in the world.

•   Your attitude can turn your pain into your passion.

•   Unpleasant circumstances in life are a common thing, but your mental attitude will determine on how you will deal with those circumstances.

•   Anger carries the spirit of revenge and if not dealt with, it can eventually turn into a venomous cancer in your heart.

•   Bitterness has the potential to weaken your immune system; to make you lose your appetite; to destroy relationships and friendships; and to create unnecessary enemies.

•   Trials of life will happen to everyone, but how you respond or react to those trials will determine how quickly you will be able to recover and move.

•   Our world and society is already full of bitterness, anger, strive and hostility, but you do have the ability to add a drop of hope into the lives of those who are hurting.

Candace Lightner took her pain and focused it toward a better goal. Likewise, we can also take our bitter circumstances and turn them into hopeful opportunities, by re-adjusting our attitude.

Attitude Questions to Consider

1. How has bitterness rewarded you in your life so far?
2. Has your bitterness or anger brought you closer to others or further away?
3. When was the last time you gave someone hope?
4. Are you contributing to our society's bitterness or its betterment?

Chapter 16

FRAGILE OR FIRM?

You Hurt My Feelings

I would love to get a little politically incorrect here with my hardcore terminologies, but I'll just stick to business without trying to offend anyone! It's no secret that we are living in very interesting times where many folks are offended by just about anything. You look at them the wrong way and they get offended. You speak out for what you personally believe in, and they get offended. And when all the crap hits the fan, they want to press charges or get you fired or your business shut down, demand policy changes, complain to their superiors, have a cry-in or riot in the streets so the whole world can feel sorry for them. So much for keeping my thoughts low-key, huh?

Anyway, fragility and firmness don't get along, and we all possess both of those attributes. The key focus here is that the world that we live in is full of it, and it's almost impossible to avoid it.

I'm a very optimistic individual, and I believe the upcoming generation has enormous potential. But I'm also very concerned for the future of our country! Why? Because we are witnessing a fragile generation which cannot handle a little heat, called reality. That's why so many people call them "snowflakes."

In one of my leadership curriculums that I have written, I have a lesson titled, "Your Growth and Maturity Will Be Tested by Fire." Your attitude will also be tested by fire. Here are the melting and boiling points of several common substances; figuratively speaking, how much does it take to make you melt or your blood to boil?

- *Water* boils at 212 degrees Fahrenheit.
- *PVC* melts at 350 degrees Fahrenheit.
- *Wood* combusts at around 450 degrees Fahrenheit.
- *Gold* melts at 1,950 degrees Fahrenheit.
- *Granite* melts at 2,300 degrees Fahrenheit.
- *Steel* melts at 2,500 degrees Fahrenheit.
- *Tungsten* melts at 6,200 degrees Fahrenheit. (Tungsten is used as a filament for light bulbs.)

Each of the above elements has a unique purpose, function and value. This is also true for every living human being. Our lives will be tested by fire; your attitude will determine whether you endure it or burn to the ground.

Shortly after my first child was born, someone said, "Whenever your child gets hurt, whether slightly or seriously, don't panic. The child senses your emotions, so try to focus them away from the pain instead of continually pointing it out." This has worked almost flawlessly with all three of my children—not because I'm some kind of super-parent, but because my attitude posture, which allowed my child to find security and assurance in me. This has also helped me in other endeavors.

This was also true for our next individual, who stood firm during one of our histories darkest hours.

THE LIFE ATTITUDE OF PRESIDENT FRANKLIN D. ROOSEVELT

Franklin D. Roosevelt is the only president in U.S. history to serve four four-year terms—and he spent most of that time confined to a wheelchair. He led the United States through the Great Depression and World War II.

While on vacation in the summer of 1921, the thirty-nine-year-old Roosevelt fell ill with polio, a disease with no known cure. He was eventually paralyzed from the waist down and underwent years of painstaking physical rehabilitation trying to regain the use of his legs. FDR would remain in the wheelchair for the rest of his life, unable to bathe or dress himself. The public never knew the full extent of his disability, however, partly because the media rarely mentioned it and in most photographs he was seated.

When FDR took office in 1933, he acted swiftly to stabilize the economy and provide jobs to those who were suffering during the Great Depression. FDR instituted new projects and programs, which were called the New Deal; they permanently changed the federal government's relationship with the U.S. populace.

In 1941, the Japanese bombed Pearl Harbor, drawing the U.S. into the Second World War. The war effort resulted in a major industrial boom, which eventually ended The Great Depression by stimulating the U.S. economy.

"The only thing we have to fear," Roosevelt once said, "is fear itself." Franklin D. Roosevelt's presidential posture and attitude without a doubt paved a way for him to be the only four-term president.

Attitude Principles To Consider

•   Be active, not reactive, since life will throw you many curveballs.

•   In life there are many ways of moving forward, but only one way of standing still. And standing still will never achieve anything.

•   FDR once said, "Men are not prisoners of fate, but only prisoners of their own minds."

•   As furnace fire reveals the quality of gold, so adversity and challenges will reveal your attitude.

•   Be willing to fight for your beliefs and convictions; no one else will do it for you.

•   Fiery trials are not meant to destroy you, but only help you to discover who your identity and potential.

•   The barrier to success is made of fear and doubt.

•   Be firm in your decisions; be firm in your convictions; and be firm in your identity.

Franklin D. Roosevelt's attitude of firmness during America's and the world's darkest hours definitely places him on the list of the best presidents in American history. It's no wonder that he once said, "When you reach the end of your rope, tie a knot in it and hang on." Likewise, we can also be firm in our attitude and not allow anyone to place a sign around our necks that reads, *I'm sensitive*.

Attitude Questions to Consider

1. Are you a fighter or a complainer?

2. How far will you go with a fragile attitude?

3. Are you willing to stand for something you strongly believe in?

4. Is your current mental attitude full of conviction or anxiety?

Chapter 17
<u>TRIALS OR TRIUMPHS?</u>
Life Happens

The truth is this, life happens! We have become experts at forecasting the weather, predicting election results, choosing the winning team, or even guessing the next jackpot, but no one has yet become an expert in forecasting the trials of life.

There is a big difference between a trial and a common problem. Trials come like a tidal wave without any warning and leave a devastating impact, while everyday problems come and go. In this chapter, I want to focus on how trials impact us in a negative way and how triumphs affect us positively.

Do you have the attitude of a victim or a victor? Are you constantly focused on your current trial, or are you trying to re-adjust your focus on the triumphs that you will achieve through it?

Trials can last a while and will definitely leave a scar. But we need to stop looking at where we have been and start looking at where we can be. The next individual has done exactly that.

THE LIFE ATTITUDE OF NICK VUJICIC

The life story of Nick Vujicic will shock you; amaze you; challenge you; kick you hard in the butt; and maybe even make you cry! He was born with tetra-amelia disorder—a rare condition where the person has no limbs at all. (In fact, he's one of only seven people worldwide who currently has it. Vujicic has two small, deformed feet, one of which he calls his "chicken drumstick" because of its shape.) When he was born, his mother refused to see or hold him, but she and her husband eventually accepted their son's condition and understood it as "God's plan" for him.

When he was eight, Vujicic could not see a bright future ahead and became depressed. When he was ten years old, he decided to end his life by drowning himself in a bathtub. After a couple of attempts, he realized he didn't want to leave his loved ones with the burden and guilt that would result from his suicide. When he was fifteen, he sealed his faith in God—and from there, life has been an amazing journey for him.

Vujicic flourished in his teenage and young adult years despite being bullied. When he was seventeen, a janitor at his high school inspired him to start speaking about his faith and how to overcome adversity; over the next two years, he spoke a dozen times to small groups. In 2005, Vujicic founded Life Without Limbs, an international non-profit ministry. And in 2007, he founded Attitude is Altitude, a secular motivational speaking company.

He graduated with a Bachelor of Commerce degree at the age of twenty-one from Griffith University in his native Australia, with a double major in financial planning and accounting.

Though Vujicic doesn't have any limbs, he has two toes on his left foot, which allow him to write and to type forty-five words per minute. He can also float in water, swim, and can even hold his breath for more than two minutes. He plays golf and soccer, operates a motor boat, and has gone sky diving, scuba diving, and surfing. He has been also able to use his foot to operate an electric wheelchair, a computer, and a mobile phone.

Vujicic was often concerned about getting married and the possibility that he might pass tetra-amelia syndrome to his future children. But miracles do happen; in 2011, he proposed to his wife Kanae, slipping the engagement ring onto her finger with his mouth. The Vujicic's now have four children—all of whom are healthy and have all of their limbs, hands, feet, fingers and toes.

Vujicic has traveled to more than sixty countries so far, and has spoken to millions of people from all walks of life. He often says he keeps a pair of shoes in his closet, just in case God decides to give him legs. He once said, "Dream big my friend and never give up. We all make mistakes, but none of us are mistakes ... Embrace the positive attitudes, perspectives, principles and truths I share, and you too will overcome."

Attitude Principles To Consider

• Your unique challenges could open up unique opportunities for you.

• "I know for certain that God does not make mistakes, but he does make miracles," Vujicic said once. "I am one. You are, too."

• Life may not be fair, but you can always find hope if you have the right attitude.

• Happiness is a choice. So is staying miserable.

- If you haven't received your miracle yet, then work on becoming a miracle for someone else.
- The challenges and difficulties of life are only here to strengthen you.
- Triumphs and victory do not come automatically, but only through perseverance and the right mental attitude.
- Do not run away from your trials, since you never know what adventures opportunity could open up through that specific trial.
- Nick Vujicic once said, "If God can use a man without arms and legs to be His hands and feet, then He will certainly use any willing heart!"

Nick Vujicic's attitude is without a doubt triumphant, and likewise we also can express many triumphant moments in our life, if we just choose to have the right mental attitude.

Attitude Questions to Consider

1. Are your trials currently hindering you from experiencing triumphs?
2. Are you proactive or reactive?
3. Are you shaking your fist at God or are you re-evaluating your current situation?

Chapter 18

EMPLOYMENT OR DEPLOYMENT?

Having the Spirit of an Entrepreneur

Allow me to introduce this chapter with one of the most untrue statements most of us have heard (and have probably been guilty of saying ourselves): "Go to college to get a good education so you can land a great-paying job, with security and good benefits." Yep that's it! This statement has thrown millions of potential entrepreneurs into a tailspin, including me.

Before you drop this book and start writing me hate mail, please consider this: There is nothing wrong with going to college to obtain a specific degree. Second, education is vital, especially if you are venturing into the medical sphere, engineering, or law.

But this is not the case for every occupation. For example, how many people do you know who are currently frustrated with their job? Maybe you're even one of them. Most often it's because many are not doing what their heart desires to do, even if they have a good paying job.

If I may, here's my background. I was born in the former Soviet Union while it was still under Communism, which definitely is oppressive and limits your options. When I was eight, my family came to the United States as refugees, giving us a fresh breath of hope. But I slowly fell into the J.O.B. (Just Over Broke) mindset, just like millions of other people—immigrants and natural-born citizens alike.

Here I am in the most opportunistic country in the whole world, where I can be whoever I want to be and achieve whatever my heart desires, to only be like a hamster in a wheel, punching a clock! There's nothing wrong with working hard, but I don't ever remember any of my teachers or professors challenging me to own my own business or to become an entrepreneur.

In my numerous travels throughout the USA, I have witnessed this interesting phenomenon about certain ethnic cultures. How many times have you been to an Asian restaurant where the owners spoke broken English? How many hotels have you stayed in that were managed or owned by someone of another ethnicity? How many gas stations and convenience stores are owned or managed by immigrants? Amazing, isn't it? Here we have immigrants with broken English from different walks of life who are business owners and entrepreneurs, while many folks who are natural-born citizens just have jobs!

The just-over-broke (JOB) mentality has victimized millions, including those with higher education—and as a result, we have many frustrated individuals with frustrated attitudes.

Next time you're at work, try asking your co-workers if they are happy with their current job or not? Yes, I mean all of them, which includes your supervisor and manager. What if you are the manager or the president and have people working for you? Even better! In this case you may hear some shocking truth from your employees, if they choose to tell you the truth without thinking they will be fired.

I'm reminded of a true story I read about a successful leadership consultant who had an intriguing conversation with a group of executives from Sony.

"Why is it," the consultant asked, "that whenever I travel, especially through America, I see Asians who own business like restaurants?"

After a short pause, one of the executives replied, "You know, we also were very troubled by this question. Whenever we travel around the world, and especially through America, we notice that a lot of black people are janitors." (This consultant had dark skin pigmentation).

"Well," the consultant asked, somewhat taken aback, "were you able to discover why that is so?"

"Yes," the executive said. "It's because when our people move to any part of the world, they look for a business, but your people look for a job!"

For some this may sound like an extremely offensive racial statement. The lesson here is: Are you looking for employment or deployment?

And in the following section you will be introduced to nine billionaires who had surprising beginnings.

THE LIFE ATTITUDE OF NINE BILLIONAIRES WHO DID NOT GRADUATE HIGH SCHOOL

1. John D. Rockefeller

He dropped out of high school at the age of sixteen to get a job, and later became history's first recorded billionaire. Rockefeller founded the Standard Oil Company and made billions before the government broken up his company, because they considered it to be a monopoly. Following that, he spent the last forty years of his life giving his wealth away—paradoxically, helping millions get a good education.

2. Henry Ford

Henry Ford was born into utter poverty. Formal education didn't interest him, so he quit school after the eighth grade and found satisfaction by working with his hands on complicated tasks. Ford eventually became an apprentice in a machine shop, and later chief engineer at the Edison Illuminating Company. He built his first "horseless carriage" in 1896, founding the car industry. In today's market, Ford's net worth would be estimated around $200 billion! This is definitely remarkable for someone who did not have a formal education.

3. Ray Kroc

Ray Kroc dropped out of school around the age of fifteen in order to join the army and serve his country. He spent most of his early career selling paper cups and milkshake machines. Later, he met the McDonald brothers, who purchased his milkshake machines. After witnessing the success of their restaurant and their simple menu, Kroc suggested they grow other franchise-style restaurants in different locations. The McDonald brothers were not too enthusiastic about that—so Kroc eventually bought out the restaurant with all of its rights and created the McDonalds Corporation. Today, McDonalds is considered the largest restaurant franchise, with around thirty-seven thousand restaurants spread across 120 countries and territories. Today, this corporate franchise is valued at about $14 billion.

4. Kirk Kerkorian

Kirk Kerkorian is an American businessman, investor, and philanthropist who dropped out of school in eighth grade. He was born to Armenian immigrants and didn't learn English until he began playing with street kids. At age nine, he began selling newspapers and working odd jobs.

Later in life, he purchased his first airplane, then a small airline, which was the beginning of his wealth escalation, and then built the three largest casino hotels in Las Vegas (International Hotel, MGM Grand Hotel (now Bally's Las Vegas), and MGM Grand). He also purchased the Metro-Goldwyn-Mayer movie studio, and provided over $1 billion for charity in Armenia through his Lincy Foundation. His net worth was estimated around $4 billion at the time of his death in 2015.

5. David H. Murdock

David H. Murdock dropped out of high school in the ninth grade and worked at a gas station. After serving in World War II, Murdock was homeless and poor. He managed to get a $1,200 loan to buy a diner that was closing, then flipped it and made a $700 profit. He went into real estate and mining, becoming the largest shareholder in Occidental Petroleum. In 1985, he took over the Hawaiian real estate outfit Castle & Cooke, which owned Dole Food Company. Dole became the world's largest fruit and vegetable producer. Today, Murdock is estimated to be worth around $3 billion.

6. Richard Branson

Sir Richard Branson struggled in school due to his dyslexia. At the age of sixteen, he dropped out; his teacher told him he would either end up in prison or become a millionaire. This led to him to launch Virgin Records, and then the Virgin Group, which controls more than four hundred companies. Branson's estimated net worth is about $5 billion.

7. Carl Lindner, Jr.

Carl Lindner, Jr. dropped out of school at the age of fourteen to help his family run their dairy business. Later in life, his father opened one of the nation's first cash-and-carry milk and dairy stores, which eventually became the United Dairy Farmers convenience-store chain. Lindner founded the American Financial Corporation and in 1999, he also became part owner and CEO of the Cincinnati Reds baseball team. Lindner is estimated to have a net worth of $2.3 billion.

8. James H. Clark

James H. Clark had a poverty-stricken childhood and dropped out of high school at age sixteen, because he was a boisterous troublemaker in the classroom. After spending four years in the Navy, he decided to go back to school and eventually earned his PhD. In 1981 he founded Silicon Graphics Incorporated and later on this company became the world leader in the production of Hollywood movie visual effects. Later on he co-founded Netscape (web browser), which later was bought out by AOL. Then he launched Healtheon (connecting physicians, patients, and health care institutions by eliminating unnecessary paperwork). Clark's net worth is estimated at $2.1 billion.

9. Francois Pinault

Francois Pinault dropped out of high school to work at his father's lumber mill because his classmates bullied him. After learning a few things from his father's business, he started buying smaller firms and transforming them into giant enterprises. His holding company owns Gucci, Samsonite, Puma and Kering. The Pinault family's net worth is approximately $31.5 billion.

These are just a few of the billionaires who don't have high school diplomas; I didn't even mention the multi-millionaires. Moreover, there's a slew of successful entrepreneurs who didn't finish college because they were so busy pursuing their passions—people like Mark Zuckerberg, Steve Jobs, Bill Gates, Oprah Winfrey, Michael Dell, Matt Mullenweg, Jack Taylor, and Elizabeth Holmes.

This by no means is meant to degrade academia; only to point out that a degree isn't necessary to release entrepreneurial ability. But the attitude of these nine billionaires should give everyone hope!

Attitude Principles To Consider

•   Your job should only be your practice field for being deployed into your purpose and vision.

- A person can change his future by changing his attitude.
- Laziness has never made anyone rich or successful, but only those who choose to dream big and to work intently.
- Don't just look for a job; look for an opportunity to propel you to the next level of your life.
- One way to uncover your entrepreneurial ability is to discover your inner purpose and the thing you continually dream about.
- Some of the most miserable people are financially successful. Why? Because they are stuck in a "good" job, while their heart is continually dreaming of something bigger.
- Becoming an entrepreneur does not require a lot of money, knowledge, or connections, but does require the right mental attitude and a desire to achieve greatness.
- Whatever captivates your thoughts is a sign of what you need to pursue.
- An entrepreneur dreams, while an employee fantasizes.

Great education will not guarantee you success. Knowledge will not necessarily open new doors for you. And trying to make it big through luck will leave you broken and devastated. But the day you meet yourself will be the day you discover your true purpose and passion— bringing everything else into proper alignment.

Once that happens, you will know whether you need to get a higher degree from a college or university, what type of books to read, which type of friends to have, and most importantly, which type of mentors and life coaches you need!

Don't become just another hamster on a wheel or a dumb sheep with a herd mentality. Become a dreamer and a believer, because you were born for greatness.

Attitude Questions to Consider

1. Are you looking for employment or deployment?

2. Are you looking for rights or responsibilities?

3. Do you desire to own a business or to have a great job?

Chapter 19

RISK OR SECURITY?

How Much Are You Willing to Sacrifice?

Those who have achieved greatness, broke new records, discovered new ideas and generated enormous wealth were always risk takers! The Thesaurus defines *risk* as a liability, gamble, speculation and also as an opportunity. And it defines *security* as freedom, insurance, sanctuary and shelter. What a big contrast!

Risk takers are those who are passionate about their dreams and who are willing to pay the necessary price to brings those dreams into their full fruition. And risk takers are also willing to sacrifice their personal time, their hobbies, their finances, their leisure & entertainment and even their well-being in order to do what average folks wont.

Likewise, on the flipside of things, those who prefer a risk-free environment where they feel safe and secure are not willing to go beyond average. These individuals would rather drive in the comfort zone lane on cruise control, instead of going off road though uncharted territories. And their mindset is fixed on their personal well-being on how they can be safe & secure without risking or jeopardizing their current achievements and assets.

Before I ventured out as an entrepreneur, I blindly enjoyed my comfort zone, since it gave me a sense of security. But with so much mediocrity that surrounded me on a daily basis, I got very bored and my innovative thinking became dull. I knew that I had an inner ambition to achieve greater things in life, but in those early years I have created a safety switch in my subconscious, which gave me a numbing feeling of security. But with a continual kick on my butt cheeks from my loving wife kept on challenging me to begin to release my inner potential and that of course required taking risks.

As I began to reflect back on some of my greater breakthroughs and achievements, I have witnessed a similar pattern and that pattern had to do with me taking risks. When I would get out of my comfort zone, and began venturing out into new territories, only then I experienced greater achievements and success. This resulted in my inner gratification of life.

But now I want to divert your focus to two unique individuals who sacrificed and risked much, and as a result have obtained much honor and favor from those who were hopeless.

THE LIFE ATTITUDE OF OSKAR SCHINDLER AND CORRIE TEN BOOM

Oskar Schindler

Oskar Schindler was born into a wealthy German Catholic family. After attending primary and secondary school, Oskar enrolled in a technical school, from which he was expelled for forging his report card. Before the Holocaust, he was a prolific drinker and was arrested several times for public drunkenness.

Schindler joined the Nazi Party in order to capitalize on the war after he began to sense the shift in political momentum, and eventually became a spy. He was arrested by Czech authorities in 1938 and sentenced to death, but was released when Germany annexed the Sudetenland.

While looking for business opportunities, he quickly became involved in the black market. Schindler used his charm to bribe high-ranking German officers with gifts. Eventually he purchased an enamel factory, starting out with forty-five employees, but the company grew to more than 1,700 at its peak.

When Schindler saw the horrendous torture and murder the Jews were experiencing in the Plaszow concentration camp, he was moved to save those he could. In the beginning, he hid Jewish investors in exchange for money—but then started providing refuge for others, regardless of money, as the Nazis increasingly hunted them down.

As time went on, Schindler was forced to give Nazi officials ever-larger bribes and more luxurious gifts to keep them from inspecting his factory and to keep his Jewish workers safe.

After spending millions protecting Jews, he went bankrupt in 1958. Schindler spent the rest of his life supported by donations from the Schindlerjuden. He was also named a Righteous Gentile by Yad Vashem (Monument and Holocaust Remembrance Center) in 1962, and after his death in 1974, Schindler was interred in the Catholic cemetery on Mount Zion in Jerusalem. In 1993, director Steven Spielberg brought the story of Oskar Schindler to the big screen with his film *Schindler's List*, which was nominated for seven Academy Awards. He saved 1,200 lives.

Corrie ten Boom

Corrie ten Boom and her devoutly religious family helped Jews escape the Nazi Holocaust during World War II. Faith inspired them to offer shelter, food and money to those in need. But in 1940, the German Blitzkrieg ran through the Netherlands, and their quiet life was changed forever.

During the war, their house became a refuge for Jews. A secret room, no larger than a small wardrobe closet, was built into ten Boom's bedroom behind a false wall. It could hold up to six people, all of whom had to stand quiet and still. When periodic security sweeps came through their neighborhood, a buzzer in the house signaled danger, which gave the refugees only a few minutes to hide. Over the next few years, they saved about 800 Jews.

On February 28, 1944, a Dutch informant told the Nazis of the ten Booms' activities, and the Gestapo raided their home. Even though the entire ten Boom family was arrested, the German soldiers didn't find the half-dozen Jews safely concealed in the hiding place. All the ten Boom family members were incarcerated in February 1944.

Corrie was initially held in solitary confinement for three months, and later was sent to a political concentration camp. Despite the brutal conditions, the murder of prisoners, and abuse from the guards, ten Boom ministered to women in the camp, sharing the Gospel from a small Bible that was smuggled in.

On Christmas Day, 1944, she was released. Afterward, she found out her release was due to a clerical error; a week later, all the women in her age group were sent to the gas chambers.

In 1946, she founded a worldwide ministry that took her to more than sixty countries. In 1971, she wrote a best-selling book of her experiences, *The Hiding Place*. In 1975, the book was made into a movie. Corrie ten Boom lived to the ripe old age of 91. She once said, "This is what the past is for! Every experience God gives us, every person He puts in our lives, is the perfect preparation for the future that only He can see."

Attitude Principles To Consider

• Taking risks will set you on a adventurous path, while choosing to be secure will make your life dull.

• Corrie ten Boom once said, "In order to realize the worth of the anchor, we need to feel the stress of the storm."

• Let us learn how to sacrifice today so the next generation can have a better tomorrow.

• Risk takers had their names engraved into the history books, while security makers came and vanished just like the wind.

• Ordinary individuals are willing to sacrifice others for their own well-being, while extra-ordinary individuals are willing to sacrifice themselves for the well-being of others.

• The ingredients for an adventurous and a successful life are: 1 table spoon of *desire*; 2 table spoons of *hard work ethic*; and full cup of *risk*.

• One of the dangers in life is to be in the safe-zone. Why? Because the safe-zone will never allow you to discover who you truly are.

Oskar Schindler's and Corrie ten Boom's attitude of love and sacrificial servanthood should make you speechless! This is also true with any information that comes your way, whether positive or negative. You are the doorkeeper of your mind and your life—whether you choose to take risks or simply stay in the shadows of security.

Therefore, don't allow just anyone to dump whatever they want into your life, manipulate you to see what they want you to see, make you feel what they want you to feel, or make you believe what they believe in. The antidote for getting out of your security zone is to begin taking risks without being distracted by your internal fears and doubts and by tuning out those who try to convince you that being in the safety zone in more pleasant.

Attitude Questions to Consider

1. Are you a risk taker or a security maker?
2. When was the last time you took a risk as a leap of faith?
3. Is the word *sacrifice* part of your subconscious vocabulary?
4. Are you preparing or procrastinating?

Chapter 20

DEATH OR LIFE?

The Power of Your Words

*D*eath and life are in the power of the tongue, and those *who love it will eat its fruit*, said a wise king named Solomon. Your words carry weight and power; you would be fooling yourself to think otherwise.

We don't teach babies how to cry, how to sleep, or how to smile, since those are natural human instincts that God has given us. But we invest enormous amounts of time in trying to teach them how to speak, spell and write.

The hours that parents and teachers invest in a child's early years is mindboggling! Why? Because this is a very important development process in any human being. But as adults, we tend to see the opposite taking place: We begin to steer away from the importance of words and the power and value they possess. Words and their motive behind them are powerful.

It's interesting that whenever we smell something bad or hear vulgar language in public, it makes us uncomfortable—and for a very good reason. It's the same when we're forced to deal with someone else's negative words or stinking attitude.

There is power in our words! Words have the ability to heal or to destroy. Words can clothe a person with dignity or strip them down to the bone. Words can give hope to the hopeless, or fuel a raging fire of anger and hatred. Words have the ability to entertain and amuse us, or leave us speechless in dismay.

We use words to express our love and affection for the ones we cherish. The right words are helpful during hospital visits or funerals. And words carry an endless ability to keep us attached to a particular book, an article, a poem, or a quote spoken by someone who lived hundreds of years ago.

Yes, words are important, and they are very powerful. In the following section you will learn about eight historical figures who used words as either tools or weapons.

THE LIFE ATTITUDE OF EIGHT HISTORICAL INFLUENTIAL FIGURES

Below is a handful of some of the most influential figures throughout history who used their words to great effect—both positively and negatively.

1. Aristotle

Aristotle's intellectual range was vast and rich, covering science and the arts—biology, botany, chemistry, ethics, logic, metaphysics, music, philosophy, physics, poetry, politics, psychology, and zoology.

Aristotle was a student of the Greek philosopher Plato, and was the first person in history to classify different animals. He was the founder of zoology, and made many contributions to physics. He was the first to write a book that dealt with the specifics of psychology and made many advances in meteorology. Aristotle also founded the world's first great library, where he gave lectures.

He made detailed observations of the world and recorded what he saw. He introduced a new way of studying, looking for clues and for proofs. Aristotle wrote numerous books and kept many notes to help teach his students. His influence on Western thought in the humanities and social sciences is largely considered supreme. He and some of his early colleagues established the concept of universities.

2. Joan of Arc

Joan of Arc, a peasant girl living in medieval France, believed God had chosen her to lead her nation to victory in its long-running war with England. She said she received visions of the Archangel Michael, Saint Margaret, and Saint Catherine of Alexandria instructing her to support Charles VII and to recover France from British domination.

With no military training, Joan convinced Prince Charles of Valois to allow her to lead a French army to the besieged city of Orléans, where it achieved a momentous victory over the British.

Joan was made a commander in the French army, but she never fought in any battles or killed anyone. She acted as an inspirational mascot with a banner in her hand. In 1430, she was captured at Compiègne by the Burgundian faction, then was tried for witchcraft and heresy; she was burned at the stake in 1431 at the age of nineteen, but later was declared a martyr and canonized as a Roman Catholic saint.

3. Mahatma Gandhi

Mahatma Gandhi was a scrawny, sickly kid and a mediocre student. He became a lawyer as an adult, but his shyness made him ineffective and he wasn't even remotely charismatic. Gandhi was traveling through South Africa on a first-class train ticket. However, a white man didn't want him sitting there, so a guard threw him out and he was beaten up by a white stagecoach.

Within a week, he was speaking out publicly on discrimination, mesmerizing crowds with his passion. After helping to change some of the discriminatory laws in South Africa, Gandhi moved back to his native India in 1915. Soon after, he began mobilizing the people to peacefully revolt against their British colonizers. Gandhi instructed Indians to boycott everything the British made, and even the British laws. "A man is but a product of his thoughts," he told the people. "What he thinks, he becomes."

Gandhi staged a twenty-four-day march to the sea, joined by hundreds of thousands of his countrymen. He was arrested and imprisoned many times; he went on seventeen separate hunger strikes, with the longest being twenty-one days. These hunger strikes were how he expressed his non-violent protest during his last imprisonment. Gandhi's tactics and influence worked, and eventually India gained its independence in 1947.

Gandhi's life was not smooth sailing, but full of turbulence. "Keep your thoughts positive because your thoughts become your words," he once said. "Keep your words positive because your words become your behavior. Keep your behavior positive because your behavior becomes your habits."

4. Adolf Hitler

Adolf Hitler was a quirky kid who left school at sixteen to become a painter in Vienna, a vocation at which he failed miserably. He wasn't a sociable person, had problems with relationships and couldn't engage in intellectual debate. In 1919, he joined the fascist German Workers' Party; it only took him two years to become its leader.

It was the perfect storm for him, since Germans had gotten thrashed in World War I and were poor, starving, and humiliated by the terms of their surrender. During this time Hitler railed against democracy, told the Germans they were Aryans and better than everyone else, and spoke out against their true enemies, namely Communists and Jews.

Hitler had a clear vision, and was determined to convince everyone of his mission. Millions of Germans, predisposed to hear such a message, fell for it, viewing Hitler almost like a god. In his book *Mein Kampf (My Struggle),* Hitler wrote, "I know that men are won over less by the written than by the spoken word, that every great movement on this earth owes its growth to great orators and not to great writers."

People were willing to follow him because he seemed to have the right answers in a time of enormous economic upheaval. In more than five thousand persuasive speeches, this Nazi leader bewitched his audiences and promised them that his empire would reign for a thousand years. It didn't; but it was responsible for the extermination of six million Jews, a blight on his nation's history that has yet to be erased.

5. Alexander the Great

Alexander the Great is perhaps the greatest military genius of ancient times; he conquered the world by the age of thirty-two. He was taught by Aristotle from the time he was thirteen.

He was charismatic, ruthless, brilliant, hungry for power, diplomatic, and bloodthirsty. His men would follow him anywhere and, if necessary, die in the process. While Alexander was riding up the battle lines, he would address the soldiers with words that suited various situations. "I am not afraid of an army of lions led by a sheep," he once said. "I am afraid of an army of sheep led by a lion." This statement encouraged his soldiers, since they acknowledged him as a lion-like leader.

Alexander reminded his soldiers many times that his enemies could have taken his life, but by the grace and providence of the gods, he was still preserved. "With the right attitude," he said, "self-imposed limitations vanish." In his fifteen years of conquest, Alexander never lost a battle.

6. William Tyndale

William Tyndale was a gifted linguist and scholar, known as a man of virtue and good character, who was influenced by ideas of the Reformation and became known as a man of unorthodox and radical religious views. Tyndale was keen to translate the Bible into English. He believed this would help ordinary people understand Scripture directly and not through the filter of the Catholic Church.

Tyndale was fed up with the religious legalism and hypocrisy of the established church system of his day. He once boldly stated, "I defy the Pope and all of his laws. If God spare my life, ere many years I will cause a boy who drives the plough to know more of the scriptures than you do."

He was very concerned for his fellow man, and longed for them to personally understand the truths of the Bible. "I perceived how that it was impossible to establish the lay people in any truth except the Scripture were plainly laid before their eyes in their mother tongue."

His most revolutionary act—translating the Bible into English—is still felt today, more than five hundred years later. It also ensured he was eventually executed for heresy.

7. William Shakespeare

William Shakespeare could be considered one of the greatest early pioneers of drama, acting and entertainment. Few people realize Shakespeare was also an actor who performed in many of his own plays, as well as those of other playwrights.

During his life Shakespeare performed before Queen Elizabeth I and, later, King James I, who was a passionate fan of his work. Shakespeare wrote thirty-eight plays, 154 sonnets and a number of poems. He collaborated on several others.

Although Shakespeare is considered one of the finest writers of the English language, his generation wasn't always impressed with his work. However, the *Oxford English Dictionary* tells us he introduced almost three thousand new words to the English language. It has been estimated that his vocabulary ranged from seventeen thousand to twenty-nine thousand words!

Also, according to the *Oxford Dictionary of Quotations*, Shakespeare wrote close to a tenth of the most quoted lines ever written or spoken. According to the *Literature Encyclopedia*, Shakespeare is the second-most quoted English writer after the authors of the Bible. Some of his greatest plays include *Hamlet, Macbeth, King Lear, Othello*, and *Romeo and Juliet*.

8. Jesus

Judea-Christian history records the power and the influence that Jesus illustrated, while he lived on this earth, which resulted in the birth of the Christian faith, which is also the largest religious group and movement with an estimate of 2.3 billion follower's world-wide. You don't have to be a person of faith or of any religious background to agree with the fact that throughout history we had certain figures that carried an influential message of life, hope, purpose and the pursuit of happiness, which resulted in powerful movements.

Jesus spoke numerous powerful words and statements like, *"I am the way, the truth and the live."* And his words, actions and deeds captivated people of his time and even two thousand years later, they still captivate and transform the lives of millions around the world. His manuscript, the Bible still continues to be the number one selling and distributed book world-wide. The words from the Bible are used in weddings, at funerals, cited in numerous books and in movies, and highly quoted by speakers and influential figures.

Words do have power and influence, for better or for worse. Words can bring life or death. Words can provide hope or inflict despair. Words are like water to the parched soil and words are like gasoline to a raging fire. But, you are always in control of your words and what you do with them and how you use them!

Attitude Principles To Consider

• People are not listening to your words, but they are listening to your heart.

• Your heart attitude will determine if your words will become a tool or a weapon.

• Your words will either attract friends or enemies.

• Words are like seeds and the brain is the soil, but your attitude is the hand that plants that seed.

• Do not be wise in your own eyes, but stay humble. As a result, your speech will be seasoned and fruitful to others.

• Deceitful and lying lips are like a noose; it's just a matter of time before you get caught in it.

• Whoever is able to discipline and guard his mouth will keep himself out of trouble.

• A wise person stores up much knowledge and wisdom, but the mouths of fools lead them and others to destruction.

Decide today to sow your words like a potential seed into the hearts and lives of others, so in due time those seeds will sprout and bring forth a pleasant harvest. It does not require power or authority or status or higher education or even much knowledge to re-adjust the attitude of your heart in order to bring captivate the hearts of others.

Attitude Questions to Consider

1. Do your words bring life, hope and encouragement, or death, devastation and dismay?
2. Will your words and deeds go to the grave with you or live on in the hearts and minds of others?
3. Do your words make you a fool before others or someone whom they want to listen to and follow?

Chapter 21
DAM OR RIVER?
The Power of Servanthood

The Hoover Dam was the largest dam in the world at the time of its completion. It took about five years to build this gigantic concrete wall that holds ten trillion gallons of water; that's enough to cover the whole state of Connecticut in ten feet of water!

Dams are manmade, while rivers are a natural product of our ecosystem. As human beings, we have the ability to behave like either one of them: We can let our skills, knowledge, abilities, talents and purpose flow naturally into the world—or we can hold it all back.

Our attitude often becomes a subconscious mental filter, which operates like a dam. Because of this, we constrain our potential and abilities, and those around us are never able to discover who we are or the untapped treasure that lies within us. So we must discover our passion, and then allow it to flow through us like a living river.

Our next person decided to release her inner potential in the area of servanthood, and became a river of living water to the neediest people.

THE LIFE ATTITUDE OF MOTHER TERESA
Mother Teresa, whose birth name was Agnes Gonxha Bojaxhiu, was born into a middle-class Albanian family living in Macedonia. By age twelve, she knew she

would commit herself to a religious vocation. When she was eighteen, she moved to Ireland and a year later, she transferred to the Sisters of Loreto convent in Darjeeling, India.

She took her vows as a nun in 1931, choosing the name Teresa to honor Saint Therese of Lisieux. Teresa began teaching history and geography at St. Mary's High School for girls from wealthy families in Calcutta, India.

But on September 10, 1946, Mother Teresa experienced a second calling—the "call within a call"—that would forever transform her life: She said Christ spoke to her and told her to leave her teaching to work in the slums of Calcutta, aiding the city's poorest and sickest people. It took her more than a year to get official permission to leave her convent in order to pursue this new mission.

Teresa's first year in the slums was particularly hard, since she had no income and no way to obtain food and supplies other than begging on the streets. She was often tempted to return to the convent, but relied on her faith daily.

One of her first projects was to teach the children of the poor. Since she didn't have any equipment or supplies at the time, she taught them to read and write by writing in the dirt with sticks. Teresa also taught the children basic hygiene. Word soon began to spread about Mother Teresa's good works, and soon she had other volunteers wanting to help her.

During her humanitarian missions, Mother Teresa suffered from injuries and numerous diseases. She had malaria, pneumonia, suffered two heart attacks, and broke her collar bone.

During her life, Mother Teresa received more than 120 honors and awards, including one from Pope John XXIII in 1971 and the 1979 Nobel Peace Prize. To everyone's surprise, she refused the traditional banquet honoring Nobel laureates, instead requesting that the $192,000 be given to help the poor of India.

Mother Teresa was fluent in five languages (Bengali, Albanian, Serbian, English, and Hindi). Even though she was admired by the world, she was also heavily criticized for her stern stance against abortion. After her death in 1997, Mother Teresa's letters revealed that she spent almost fifty years in a crisis of faith, sometimes even doubting God's existence. But her passionate deeds were always visible. "The biggest disease today," she once said, "is not leprosy or tuberculosis, but rather the feeling of being unwanted."

Mother Teresa should not be looked upon as a divine angelic being, but as an ordinary person who decided to do extraordinary things. History remembers those who have touched and affected the lives of others in a radical way.

Attitude Principles To Consider

•	Mother Teresa once said, "I have found the paradox, that if you love until it hurts, there can be no more hurt, only more love."
•	There are no walls around the human spirit, no barriers to your progress, and no constraints to the human mind except those you erect yourself.
•	Love, mercy, and compassion don't make you look sexy outwardly, but in reality, they will make you stand out from the rest of the crowd.

• You may not control what happens to you, but you can definitely control your attitude about what happens to you. And you have the ability to master change rather than allowing it to master you.

• "We ourselves feel that what we are doing is just a drop in the ocean," Mother Teresa said. "But the ocean would be less because of that missing drop."

• We need to spread love and servanthood everywhere we go. Let no one ever come to you without leaving happier.

• It is almost impossible to genuinely serve others if you do not have love as your primary motive.

• Loving your neighbor as you love yourself is a universal principle. If we can start with that, then our world will definitely be a different place.

• The greatest pain any human being can experience is not the pain of losing a job or a lack of finances or being poor or hungry; it is the pain of not being loved or wanted.

• Often our ego, selfishness, and pride hinder us from serving others. But when we are in a desperate need and no one reaches out to us, we become angry at the whole world. It's time for an attitude adjustment!

Mother Teresa's attitude of love, mercy, compassion and servanthood definitely made her a living river that brought life and hope into the lives of the world's poor and needy. We may not be able to live up to her standards, but we can definitely take away tremendous lessons that should challenge us to be flowing rivers instead of dams.

The power of servanthood has the ability to heal the brokenhearted, to give hope to the hopeless, to bring life in the areas that are saturated with death and to give you the opportunity to partake in the suffering of others.

Attitude Questions to Consider

1. What does it mean to love until it hurts?

2. When was the last time you genuinely served someone?

3. Are you willing to serve, or only to be served?

4. Are you willing to volunteer yourself, or only to send someone else?

Chapter 22

DESTRUCTION OR CONSTRUCTION?

Are You a Victim or a Victor?

Are you constructive or destructive? Are you building or demolishing? Are you adding value to others or devaluing them?

I once heard a parable which goes something like this: A pedestrian passing by a construction site asked one of the workers, "What are you doing?"

The guy replied, "I'm working."

The pedestrian asked another worker the same question.

"I'm laying bricks," he said.

"And what are you doing?" he asked a third worker.

"I'm building a great cathedral," he said.

These three individuals were doing the exact same thing, but all had a different attitude about it.

Here's another illustration. Two rams crossing a river met in the middle of a log that had fallen across it. Which one crossed over safely? Neither, because they butted heads and both fell into the river! In the same way, our attitude of adding value to others or operating out of selfishness and ego will determine how successfully we arrive at our destination in life.

Our next individual understood the importance of not being a victim, but built up people who had been victimized for generations.

THE LIFE ATTITUDE OF DR. MARTIN LUTHER KING, JR.

He was born as Michael King, Jr. in Atlanta, Georgia, but later both he and his father changed their names to Martin Luther, after the German Protestant leader. King was such a gifted student that he skipped high school completely and entered college at the age of fifteen, attending Morehouse College, Crozer Theological Seminary, and Boston University, where he received his doctorate.

When Rosa Parks refused to give up her seat to a white man on a bus, it sparked a year-long bus boycott. Within days, the Montgomery Improvement Association was founded to coordinate the boycott, and King was elected president of the organization. King's house was bombed while he was at a meeting. His wife and daughter were home at the time, but luckily were uninjured. When the U.S. Supreme Court ruled the bus segregation laws unconstitutional, the boycott ended and King emerged as a national civil rights leader.

In 1957, The Southern Christian Leadership Conference (SCLC) was established in Atlanta, with King as president. He went on to lead monumental freedom marches all over the segregated South—including one in Birmingham, Alabama, where he was arrested. During the March on Washington for Jobs and Freedom in 1963, King delivered his famous "I Have a Dream" speech on the steps of the Lincoln Memorial, and was later named *Time* magazine's Man of the Year.

On July 2, 1964, King stood behind President Lyndon B. Johnson as he signed the Civil Rights Act of 1964 into law. That same year, King won the Nobel Peace Prize, which made him the youngest person ever to win it up to that point. A year later, President Johnson signed the Voting Rights of 1965, giving black people the right to vote.

Over the next few years, King's influence and popularity increased—but not with everyone. On April 4, 1968, he was assassinated in Memphis, Tennessee, by James Earl Ray.

In 1977, King was posthumously awarded the Presidential Medal of Freedom by President Jimmy Carter. In 1980, the Martin Luther King, Jr. Historic Site opened in Atlanta. And in 1983, President Ronald Reagan declared King's birthday a federal holiday, to be observed annually on the third Monday in January—making King the only non-president to have national holiday in his name.

In 1991, The National Civil Rights Museum opened at the site of the Lorraine Motel in Memphis, where King was assassinated. And in 2006, the groundbreaking ceremony for the Martin Luther King, Jr. National Monument in Washington, D.C. took place—the first monument on the National Mall dedicated to an African-American.

From 1957 to 1968, King traveled more than six million miles and spoke more than 2,500 times. He was arrested twenty-nine times, assaulted four times, and nearly assassinated ten years before his death. King was awarded twenty honorary degrees and authored six books; there are approximately nine hundred streets and more than one hundreds schools named after him nationwide. What a remarkable historical figure King was!

Attitude Principles To Consider

• The measure of who you are is not where you stand in moments of convenience and comfort, but where you stand in times of challenge, controversy, and chaos.

• The time is always now to do what is right, even when all the odds are against you.

• The day you become blind to those who are suffering is the day your life on earth becomes useless.

• Love for your fellow man can transform an enemy into a friend.

• Your words and deeds are capable of building skyscrapers or digging graves.

• There is a price to pay for freedom, but apathy will eventually cost you a lot more.

• Fight with conviction, speak with passion, and have a constructive attitude for success.

• Your attitude comes from your belief system.

• Love is a powerful tool that can achieve the impossible, while hatred is a powerful force that can wreak immeasurable destruction.

• Never allow others to define you.

Martin Luther King Jr's attitude was not of a victim, but a victor, which gave him the bravery and the boldness to stand up for civil rights. King once said, "If a man has not discovered something that he will die for, he isn't fit to live." With such a powerful statement like that, we should all lay aside our victimhood mentality by changing our attitude towards our self; towards others; and towards the betterment of our society, as we choose to be constructive and not destructive.

Attitude Questions to Consider

1. Are you a demolitionist or a builder?

2. Are you willing to pay a price for something that you strongly and passionately believe in?

3. Are you responding to problems or reacting to them?

4. Are you an agent of change or a victim of change?

Chapter 23

GIVE UP OR GROW UP?

Are You Going Through Life or Growing Through Life?

Lately, I've been going through hell and high water, but thank God I'm still standing. Here is one personal example: Me and my family moved to the state of Georgia back in 2013 and on the day of our arrival I discovered that my debit card was being declined when I was trying to fill my car with gas. After accessing my online bank account, I realized the my checking account was completed withdrawn, and was also left with a negative balance. When I called the bank, they said that the IRS has placed a levy on my account. So, here we are in our new residence, in a new state, and with a insufficiency of two-thousand dollars.

Thank God, that I had about $700 dollars in cash with me, until I received my next paycheck. But the next three-year battle with the IRS and about a hundred wasted hours into numerous phone calls (talking & on-hold), and also writing letters to so many different department agencies did burst my bubble many times. Eventually, the IRS refunded my money due to their error, but the hefty damage was already done, which affected our credit score, and we were also not able to get any personal or business bank loans.

Though our transitional season still isn't quite over, my attitude—as well as my wife's has played a vital role in getting through it.

Giving up is easy—but that only brings more frustration and bitterness. So we can either give up—or grow up. To be successful, you will have to face many lonely battles. This is not easy, but it is necessary in order for you to discover your full potential. As you grow, so does your potential.

It's often during the darkest seasons of our life that we are able to grow the most. Our next individual faced a dark era that swept through Europe, but had the right attitude to overcome.

THE LIFE ATTITUDE OF WINSTON CHURCHILL

As a student, Winston Churchill performed poorly in virtually every subject. Even though Churchill is well known now for his speeches, he suffered from a speech impediment all his life.

Churchill became a war correspondent during Northwest Frontier. In 1899, his armored train was ambushed and he was captured and marched to a prison camp in South Africa. He soon escaped by scaling a wall at night, even as two of his fellow prisoners turned back. His daring escape earned him instant fame. During World War I, Churchill, who was a Lord of the Admiralty, organized a massive attack against the Ottoman Empire that failed miserably, because of defeat and much casualties; as a result, he lost his admiralty post.

Churchill was extremely prone to accidents. He once jumped off a bridge and suffered a ruptured kidney, as well as a concussion. Later on, he nearly drowned in a Swiss lake, and fell several times from horses. When he was learning to fly, he crashed a plane. And while in the United States in 1931, Churchill was hit by a car in New York City because he failed to look both ways when crossing a street. But none of these incidents slowed him down; he lived to the age of 90 before dying of a stroke.

On May 10, 1940, King George VI appointed Churchill as prime minister and the minister of defense. Churchill quickly formed a cabinet of leaders from the Conservative, Liberal and Labor parties, placing intelligent and talented men in key positions.

After the United States entered World War II in 1941, Churchill was confident the Allies would win the war. In the months that followed, he worked closely with U.S. President Franklin D. Roosevelt and Soviet dictator Joseph Stalin to forge a war strategy. "We shall defend our island, whatever the cost may be," Churchill said during a BBC broadcast one night. "We shall fight on the beaches, we shall fight on the landing grounds, we shall fight in the fields and in the streets, we shall fight in the hills. We shall never surrender. …Victory at all costs, victory in spite of all terror, victory however long and hard the road may be; for without victory, there is no survival."

Churchill served two terms as Britain's prime minister, but was voted out of office before World War II ended. Not everyone liked Churchill's politics. He was heavily criticized for the use of poisonous gas; for the famine in India; for strong negative statements against

Gandhi; for his passive attitude towards the Jews; and for his military use against the union strikers.

However, he wrote more than twenty books for which he won several awards, including the 1953 Nobel Prize in literature. The government even honored him by erecting a 12-foot statue of him in Parliament Square.

World War II has definitely reshaped the whole world and those who stood boldly in the midst of this dark era can teach us all many valuable lessons.

Attitude Principles To Consider

• Winston Churchill once said, "Attitude is a little thing that makes a big difference."
• The price of greatness is responsibility.
• The difficulties you are able to master will eventually become opportunities.
• Become a change agent and a history maker.
• Measure your life not by your present circumstances, but by the quality of your thinking.
• Failure and defeat is already engraved on too many tombstones, so before you die make some kind of a difference in this world.
• The day you begin to grow up will be the day you take full control of your attitude.

Winston Churchill's attitude for resisting the Nazi invasion and Hitler's propaganda was successful, but it came at a price. The lesson he leaves us is that we need to grow through life's challenges, not just go through them. "Success," as he once said, "consists of going from failure to failure without loss of enthusiasm."

Attitude Questions to Consider

1. Are you going through life or growing through life?

2. What will history remember you for?

3. Do you have a fixed mindset or a growth mindset?

4. What will help you to achieve the impossible?

Chapter 24

<u>ME OR WE?</u>

Self-Centeredness is a Cancer

Here's a thought! If someone gave Mother Teresa $100 million, would you have a problem with that? What if the same amount of money was offered to a 14-year-old? You probably wouldn't have a problem with the first choice, but you likely would with the second. The point is: Mother Teresa had an attitude of servanthood, while the 14-year-old is living with the belief that everybody owes them a handout.

More and more, our society is being structured around the notion of *me* instead of *we*. This is extremely evident through social media, academia, liberal ideologies, politics and policies, arts and entertainment. And of course, one the biggest victims of all of this is the younger generation.

Having a teenager in your family tends to shift your perspective. My 14-year-old son bombards me with endless questions about *why* and *why* not. There's a pattern: Most, if not all, of his questions are focused on him and how it would benefit him or what he would get out of this or that! Very few pertain to the benefit of our family or his two younger sisters.

This isn't likely a surprise to any parent of a teenager. We understand this is just a normal development process every human being goes through ... but what about when we see it in older folks?

Age by itself does not make you wiser or more mature, but how you handle problems on a daily basis does. Self-centeredness isn't found just in teenagers with raging hormones, but in every age group; human beings are selfish by nature.

Years ago, I read a parable that went something like this:

A man traveling through a desert came upon a well. Sitting next to it was a bottle full of water. He grabbed the bottle, but then noticed a sign that said, "After you drink this water, please drop the bucket into the well and refill the bottle for the next person." Eventually he did!

The lesson here is that once you have quenched your thirst, it would have been a normal thing for you to just move on forward without any thoughts of others who would be in your similar dire situation. It's one thing to barely make it to the well—but if you still have enough energy to draw the water from the well without passing out or dying. In this particular scenario, someone who has proceeded before you has already refilled the water bottle. Likewise, you need to do for others what's been already done for you. Often, we are too concerned for our own well-being, and not to look out for others.

The *me, myself and I* attitude is at the basis of injustice, racism, immorality, community breakdowns, and civil unrest. But once we align our hearts in the proper focus, we can be the change agents in our society.

Our next group of individuals, whose names you likely don't know, knew what it meant to put others' needs ahead of their own.

THE LIFE ATTITUDE OF 412 EMERGENCY WORKERS

Who could ever forget the events of September 11, 2001? Of the 2,977 victims who died that day, 412 were emergency workers who responded to the World Trade Center attack by trying to save others.

-343 firefighters (including a chaplain and two paramedics) of the New York City Fire Department
-Thirty-seven officers of the Port Authority of New York and New Jersey Police Department
-Twenty-three officers of the New York City Police Department
-Eight emergency medical technicians and paramedics from private emergency medical services
-1 member of the New York Fire Patrol

No tragic event is easy to absorb, but the hopeful aspect to this one is the heroic and selfless individuals who stepped out of their comfort zones in order to save someone else's life.

We constantly hear about tragic shootings-then learn there were individuals who used their bodies to shield others. We hear about people trapped in burning buildings, then learn that someone received major burns by running in to save them. It seems like nearly every tragedy we hear about involves at least one heroic person who tries to stop it.

Attitude Principles To Consider

- Serving others is sacrificial, selfless, and often unappreciated by others.
- A self-centered person only sees themselves, their problems, and their needs, but a serving person sees others and how they can help them with their needs.
- Some of the greatest things were accomplished by individuals, not teams.
- Sacrifice and servanthood should be a lifestyle, not a single good deed.
- Self-centered people think about how others can serve them. Become an agent of change and serve others.
- Your life will not be measured by how you lived, but by what you lived for.
- Serving others without getting anything in return will keep you humble.

For the purposes of our discussion, I'm coining some new terms here: *Meattitude* and *Weattitude*.

Your attitude is like salt or sugar, which is supposed to add flavor to others. But what happens if your salt or sugar loses its flavor? This depends on whether you are focused only on yourself or if you are focused on others. The *Meattitude* binds you to your own inner world, while the *Weattitude* opens you up to the rest of the world.

Self-centeredness is rapidly devouring our society. We're so used to this that it surprises us to find out someone we know has been going through a trial that we never knew about! Self-centeredness blinds us to those in need around us—even when we're living under the same roof.

Become an agent of change, as you tune in your attitude to be people-focused and not self-centered. The *me* attitude has never brought any hope of healing to anyone, so change your attitude from *me* to *we*!

Attitude Questions to Consider

1. Are you a team player or just a player on the team?

2. Do you more often use the words "I" and "me" or "we and "you"?

3. Are you inspiring others or manipulating them?

Chapter 25
<u>FOLLOWER OR LEADER?</u>
Leadership is Influence

There are no shortcuts in forming the right attitude to become an influential person. You can read this book, or many others like it, and remain the same. You can attend numerous conferences and equipping seminars and still have a stinky attitude. You can hire a personal life coach who will do their best to implant everything they have into your head, but this will have little effect until you personally choose to discipline yourself in what you say and do, and how you react and how you restrain your emotions.

Leadership isn't reserved just for those who are charismatic, of a certain age, or who have great public speaking skills! Those all have their purpose, but are not the primary characteristics that make you an effective or influential leader.

Everyone needs at least one mentor in their life. We don't know it all, and we won't have what it takes to be a successful leader until we are able to humble ourselves and come under the mentorship of an individual who has a credible and genuine track record of success in the area we're seeking mentorship.

Our next individual has been a mentor to me, and continues to radically impact my attitude, my thinking, and my personal development in the area of leadership.

The Life Attitude Of John C. Maxwell

John C. Maxwell had a humble beginning as a twenty-something pastor who was hungry for personal growth. In 1970, he bought a leadership training kit for $799 at a seminar—which was about what he earned in a month, and something it took him six months to save enough to buy. He also offered to pay successful pastors $100 an hour to teach him their leadership skills.

As he grew, he began teaching leadership to his staff, and then to business owners. Eventually, he felt the need to leave the church ministry and go full-time into the corporate business sphere.

In 1992, he founded INJOY Stewardship, which guides churches in their fundraising efforts; to date, INJOY has served more than 4,500 churches. In 1996, Maxwell founded EQUIP Leadership, a non-profit organization specializing in training and mobilizing effective Christian leaders around the world; so far, it has developed millions of leaders in more than eighty countries. And in 2014, Maxwell was named the No. 1 leadership and management expert in the world by *Inc. Magazine*.

Maxwell has written more than eighty books (many of which have been *New York Times* best-sellers), which have sold a total of more than twenty million copies worldwide and have been translated into multiple languages. He speaks annually to Fortune 500 companies, at leadership seminars, and to international government leaders.

Why did I choose John C. Maxwell? Over the years his books, seminars, workshops and through the John

141

Maxwell Team, which I have been a member of since 2012, have been mentoring me in the area of leadership and personal growth. Leadership has become my passion and my life journey and why not have on the greatest leadership mentors of our modern day.

John Maxwell's genuine passion for personal development without having any bias against the individual's cultural, ethnic, political or religious background, is evident in both his teachings and his life.

But the one specific thing that made me want to become a continual student of John Maxwell, more than any other, is something he once said at my certification seminar: "I have written numerous, books, I have trained and spoken to millions of people around the world, and I have achieved immeasurable things in my personal life. And now being in my older age I could just simply relax and enjoy life, since I have learned so much as a leader. But, I want to say this to you that if the day ever comes when I no longer invest into my further personal development and growth, then that will be that day when I give you my permission to stop listening to me and to stop reading my material. Why, because I will have nothing new to add to your life, since I have stopped furthering my personal growth and development." And he usually adds, "The day I stop personally growing will be the day I die!"

Wow! The first time I heard him say that was at the John Maxwell Team certification seminar I attended in 2012. You could have heard a pin drop in the audience of five hundred hungry mentees from forty different countries who were there that day. That phrase was powerful. Afterward, it kept repeating itself in my mind.

If someone like him, who has achieved so much and has impacted so many people around the world is telling me that he will continue to grow until he dies, I told myself, *then I definitely have no excuse in my life.*

Maxwell once said, "People may hear your words, but they feel your attitude." Your attitude will determine whether you become an influential leader or a typical follower.

Attitude Principles To Consider

- Leaders do daily what followers do occasionally.
- You are like a paintbrush, but your attitude is the paint.
- A leader is willing to serve; followers are willing to be served.
- A leader has the mindset of a lion, while the follower has the mindset of a sheep.
- A leader will always influence others, while the follower will always be influenced by others.
- A leader leaves behind a legacy; a follower leaves behind a will.
- You have to choose what type of attitude you will have every day.
- A leader is the first one to come and the last one to leave; a follower will show up late and leave early.
- You choose to be either the master or the victim of your attitude.
- A leader focuses on fulfilling the needs of others, while the follower focuses on fulfilling his own needs.

If I can sum up all the things I have learned from Maxwell, it would be this: Never stop growing and always have the right heart attitude to serve others with your gifts and talents. Doing so, you'll help make the world a much better place. With that said, I want to challenge you my friend to become a leader just like a lion, and not a sheep who is being led to the slaughter. Your attitude of how you see yourself will make all the difference.

Attitude Questions to Consider

1. **Are you a leader or a follower?**
2. **Are you a sheep or the shepherd?**
3. **Are you leading others or managing them?**
4. **Are you building more leaders or more followers?**

Chapter 26
<u>CRITICIZE OR ANALYZE?</u>
Growth and Development Requires Pruning

Let's get a show of hands from everyone who has received criticism at some point. No one—and I mean no one—likes to receive criticism, even when it's constructive! But the purpose of criticism is to challenge us to improve who we are, what we are doing, where we are going, and what we are trying to accomplish.

Criticism is a type of fertilizer that will help you grow, if you are willing to receive it. Positive criticism is constructive and educational—but even negative criticism gives you the opportunity to check your inner identity, what you stand for, what you believe, and the vision you have for your life.

Cemeteries are full of people who resisted criticism. They shunned people who could have drawn out their hidden potential. They may have had ideas—which were not birthed; inventions—which were not developed; books which were not written or songs that we will never sing, all because they chose to avoid criticism.

Criticism is the price you pay for success. So prepare yourself for it, and then you will eventually profit from it. Criticism allows us to look deeper into a specific area of our lives to see what we're doing right or wrong, and where we need to improve. Also, criticism is a test that that will challenge who you are, why you exist and why you do what you are doing.

We actually *need* criticism and plenty of harsh critics in our life, because they will help us mature or encourage us to become better.

Six successful individuals show us how this works.

THE LIFE ATTITUDE OF SIX UNPREDICTABLY SUCCESSFUL PEOPLE

Walt Disney

In 1920, Walt Disney started his first business—and soon went out of business, because he failed to attract many customers. At age twenty-two, he was fired by a newspaper for not being creative enough. One of his early ventures, Laugh-o-Gram Studio, went bankrupt, Later, his Mickey Mouse cartoons were rejected because they were deemed "too scary for women." *The Three Little Pigs* was also turned down because it had only four characters.

But when that happened, Disney said, "We are not trying to entertain the critics. I'll take my chances with the public." Later, he observed, "All the adversity I've had in my life, all my troubles and obstacles, have strengthened me ... You may not realize it when it happens, but a kick in the teeth may be the best thing in the world for you." Disney holds the record with fifty-nine Oscar nominations.

Steve Jobs

Steve Jobs was an entrepreneur, business magnate, inventor, and industrial designer. He was adopted shortly after birth, and by the age of ten, was deeply involved in electronics; he became friends with many of the engineers who lived in his neighborhood. He dropped out of Reed

College after only one semester. In 1976, he co-founded Apple Computers in his family's garage with Steve Wozniak, and later introduced the Apple I computer.

An acrimonious relationship with Apple Computers CEO John Sculley led to Jobs being pushed out of his own company in 1985. One of the main reasons was Jobs' different vision for the Macintosh computer brand. But he rejoined Apple as CEO in 1997 and revitalized the failing company.

What started as an idea in a garage is now worth more than $900 billion, with 123,000 employees worldwide. Not bad for a college drop-out.

"Your time is limited, so don't waste it living someone else's life," Jobs said once. "Don't be trapped by dogma, which is living with the results of other people's thinking. Don't let the noise of others' opinions drown out your own inner voice."

Theodor Seuss Geisel

Theodor Seuss Geisel struggled to write a novel that publishing companies would call something other than "pure rubbish" several times. Seuss' first book *And to Think I Saw It on Mulberry Street*, was rejected by twenty-seven publishers before one accepted it. According to Geisel, as he was walking home to burn the manuscript after his twenty-seventh rejection letter, he happened to run into an old classmate who helped him find a publisher. *And to Think I Saw It on Mulberry Street* was a hit, and Geisel was never again called a failure.

He began writing under the name "Dr. Seuss" and became a legendary children's author. His books have topped bestseller lists, sold more than six hundred million copies, and been translated into twenty languages. Dr. Seuss once said, "Only you can control your future."

Bill Gates

When he was a teen, Bill Gates wrote his first computer program on a General Electric computer. He dropped out of Harvard University so he could fully devote himself to his fledgling business, Microsoft.

In 1987, Gates becomes the youngest billionaire in the U.S., worth $1.25 billion at the age of 31. "It's fine to celebrate success," he said, "but it is more important to heed the lessons of failure."

Milton Hershey

Milton Hershey's path to success was fraught with obstacles and plenty of setbacks, before his last name became synonymous with sweetness. He stopped attending public school after fourth grade; his parents moved around a lot, and decide to teach him a trade. Hershey began his candy-making journey at the age of fifteen.

His first two businesses failed and he went bankrupt. But in the early 1890s, his caramel company grew big and was very successful, with 1,300 employees. Hershey saw an even greater opportunity in chocolate. He took a risk by selling his successful caramel company to start the Hershey Chocolate Company. And as the saying goes, the rest is history.

"I didn't follow the policies of those already in the business," he said. "If I had, I would never have made a go of it. Instead, I started out with the determination to make a better nickel chocolate bar than any of my competitors made, and I did so."

Harrison Ford

Harrison Ford was a struggling actor for nine years, getting only small non-credited movie roles while working as a carpenter to support his family. A studio official once told him, "You'll never make it in this business."

By chance, Ford was hired to build cabinets at the home of director George Lucas, who recognized his acting talent and cast him in a supporting role in the film *American Graffiti* in 1973. Shortly afterward, Lucas invited him to audition for *Star Wars*; he landed the role of Han Solo, and has now had more than forty leading roles over his long and illustrious acting career.

"Some actors couldn't figure out how to withstand the constant rejection," Ford once said. "What I observed about my fellow actors was that most gave up very easily."

No one in history was born great! The price of greatness is criticism, hardships, mockery, ridicule, and setbacks. But these six unpredictably successful individuals kept going.

Attitude Principles To Consider

• Criticism is a type of fertilizer that will help you to grow, if you are willing to receive it.
• Criticism will reveal who you truly are and what you are capable of.

- If you want to be successful, embrace criticism.
- Be open to criticism, since it gives you the opportunity to learn and to grow.
- Praise could ruin you, while criticism will keep you humble and focused.
- Learn how to receive criticism like a homework assignment. And these assignments will eventually prepare you for the big test.
- Criticism can be your friend.

Critics are afraid of failure, but they also tend to speak the loudest against those who are taking risks and trying to do something new or different. Critics often have buried their inner dreams, so they become a force of opposition to dreamers and those who desire to achieve greatness.

What critics are afraid to do or to pursue in their personal life, they try to hinder those who are in pursuit of happiness or the pursuit of wealth or the pursuit of entrepreneurship or the pursuing of new breakthroughs and innovations. I've been surprised by how much criticism and ridicule I have experienced so far in life. But at a seminar I attended, someone once said, "If I type in your name into Google, will I find anything? Remember, only those who have done something in their life will be negatively criticized. Even Mother Teresa and Jesus were highly criticized by many!"

It's so true. If you have not done something to better your life—and especially to better the life of others—then no one will have anything to criticize you about. I know many people might criticize the content of this book, but I will still gladly embrace their harsh reviews on Amazon!

Most critics aren't interested in helping you improve your life or your specific area of expertise. But those who have the right heart and the right attitude (coaches, mentors, and parents), will be eager to give you constructive criticism. Believe me my friend, you will eventually discover who is interested in your personal success and who are those who will be flattening your entrepreneurial tires.

Attitude Questions to Consider

1. Are you fearful of criticism?

2. Is your attitude in criticize mode or in the analyze mode?

3. What proactive actions can you take to further your success?

Chapter 27

SKUNK OR PERFUME?

Stinking Thinking

Reality check! When was the last time you chased down a skunk so you could enjoy its irresistible aroma? Or maybe the opposite occurred: You bolted into the opposite direction. Our noses know the difference between the smell of a skunk or the sweet aroma of perfume—and the same is true of attitude. People can always tell which kind we have.

The skunk is actually a cute animal with a silky fur coat, but beneath is loaded with a foul-smelling spray. We may fool others by our exterior attributes. They might even want to pet us like a house cat—until they come in contact with our attitude.

When we come across people with bad attitudes, we feel uncomfortable because they create an unpleasant atmosphere. Over my life I have witnessed this a lot—even with friends and family members.

Remember, whatever your mind can conceive, it will eventually produce in your life. Why, because your lips are the doorway of your thoughts and feelings. Your attitude has the power to transform your environment, for better or worse.

Our next individual used his to change his environment in a good way.

THE LIFE ATTITUDE OF SAM WALTON

There are no shortcuts to success. During the Great Depression, Sam Walton and his family lived on a farm in Oklahoma. He delivered bottles of milk from the family cow to customers and also delivered newspapers in order to make ends meet. He joined JC Penney three days after graduating from the University of Missouri with a degree in economics. After World War II, with $25,000 that he borrowed from his father along with $5,000 he saved from his time serving in the Army, he bought a Ben Franklin variety store, which he later expanded into the big-box stores Walmart and Sam's Club.

Walton's ladder of success also came with a handful of setbacks and failures. Due to inexperience, he signed a lease giving his landlord 5 percent of sales, which he later learned was the highest any retailer paid for rent. When Walton's lease expired, the landlord refused to re-sign the agreement, forcing him to sell his well-established store to the landlord. Walton recalled this as the lowest point of his business life.

In less than two decades, Walton, working with his younger brother, James, came to own 15 Ben Franklin stores, but his frustration over the management of the chain, in particular the decision to ignore Walton's push to expand into rural communities, encouraged him to strike out on his own. In 1962, Walton opened his first Wal-Mart store in Rogers, Arkansas, and success came swiftly.

Today Walmart employs 2.3 million people through 5,300 outlets worldwide; its market value is about $220 billion. Walton's philosophy was simple: "There is only one boss: The customer. And he can fire everybody in the company from the chairman on down, simply by spending his money somewhere else."

Attitude Principles To Consider

• You need to celebrate your success and be able to embrace your failures.

• Vision is more scarce than finances—so have a great vision for your life and your dreams.

• To succeed in life, you need to stay in front of change and become the change agent.

• Walton said, "Exceed your customer's expectations. If you do, they'll come back over and over. Give them what they want—and a little more."

• Be passionate about your work, and soon everybody around you will catch it and wear it like a sweet smelling perfume.

• Celebrate your success, but be willing to find humor in your failures.

• If it seems that everybody is doing it one way, there's a good chance you can discover something new by going in the reverse direction.

• Show appreciation for the people around you, and with time you will accumulate honor and respect from them.

• Success is not given to you overnight, but through hard work, dedication, consistency and the right attitude.

Walton's attitude and big dreams allowed him to grow the world's largest retail empire. He understood success would take time and patience. Likewise, be willing to change your stinking thinking, by re-adjusting your attitude into a savory perfume, as you continue to dream big. And as you create the positive atmosphere around yourself, you will naturally begin to attract others to you, who will be willing to support and to help you to fulfill your dreams.

Attitude Questions to Consider

1. Are you focusing on opportunities or problems?
2. Do others want to be around you or do they flee your presence?
3. Are you complaining through the process or learning?

Chapter 28

<u>STRIKEOUT OR</u>

<u>HOMERUN?</u>

*The Difference Between a Reward and a
Participation Trophy*

In life we will have hits and misses. Plenty of strikeouts, some homeruns, and a rare grand slam. A few people who can teach us from their personal life experience would be Michael Jordan, Babe Ruth, and Thomas Edison.

Michael Jordan missed more than nine thousand shots in his career and lost three hundred games. Babe Ruth hit 714 home runs and struck out 1,330 times in his career. And Thomas Edison had a thousand unsuccessful attempts before inventing the light bulb.

You could be gifted with great athletic abilities and skills, but if your attitude is sour, you won't win. So use some simple motivational thoughts: "I can sell ice to Eskimos. I can sell sand to the desert, and I can sell ocean water to Pacific Islanders." That will properly align your attitude, which will keep you focused and motivated. You may even surprise yourself with a homerun.

Recently, we have been bombarded through the news networks, social media platforms and even through some of our political figures with the delusional notion of sharing the wealth and offering free handouts! And by doing so, we are noticing a drastic shift in the minds of many, especially in the younger generation. If this nonsense continues, then we will witness a rise of a generation who will have a *participation trophy* attitude, instead of a *rewards* attitude!

There are no participation trophies in life! Success is the reward for enduring trials, failures, and setbacks. Nine entrepreneurs can teach us about this.

THE LIFE ATTITUDE OF NINE SUCCESSFUL ENTREPRENEURS

Babe Ruth

Babe Ruth set a record for the most home runs in a season, while also striking out more than any other player in Major League Baseball. But as a child, Ruth routinely was caught wandering the dockyards, drinking, chewing tobacco, and taunting local police. His parents decided he needed more discipline than they could give him, so they sent him to St. Mary's Industrial School for Orphans, Delinquent, Incorrigible and Wayward Boys. By the time he was fifteen, Ruth showed exceptional skill both as a hitter and pitcher in baseball. His pitching initially caught the attention of Jack Dunn, the owner of the minor league Baltimore Orioles.

Around age nineteen, Ruth signed with the Boston Red Sox; while playing for them, they won three World Series titles. Ruth had a tremendous baseball career with 714 home runs 1,330 strikeouts. "It's hard to beat a person who never gives up," he once said.

Soichiro Honda

Soichiro Honda was turned down by Toyota Motor Corporation for a job, after interviewing for a job as an engineer. Figures!

But, Soichiro first started off as an uneducated motor mechanic in Tokyo at the age of fifteen, but later was turned down by Toyota Motor Corporation for a job as an engineer. Honda endured countless failures over four decades in search of success. His dedication and confidence finally paid off when he founded one of the largest automobile companies in the world, which now bears his name. He was the first Japanese citizen inducted into Detroit's Automotive Hall of Fame. To this day, Honda holds more than one hundred patents. "Success," he once said, "is 99 percent failure."

Colonel Sanders

Colonel Harland David Sanders famous secret chicken recipe was rejected 1,009 times before a restaurant accepted it. But before he became famous for his chicken, Colonel Sanders was a pretty good cook by the age of seven. He dropped out of seventh grade and went to live and work on a nearby farm in Indiana. At age thirteen, he left home by himself.

Later in life, Sanders falsified his birth date in order to enlist in the U.S. Army in 1906. He eventually became an honorary colonel. Before hitting it big in the fast-food industry, Sanders practiced law, operated a steamboat ferry, sold life insurance, automobile tires, and lamps, and even delivered babies.

Sanders opened his first cafe serving chicken, ham and steak dishes inside a gas station in Kentucky. For most of his life, he was a terrible businessman—but today there are more than 21,400 Kentucky Fried Chicken restaurants worldwide.

The Wright Brothers

The Wright Brothers' first five flight attempts were not measured in miles, but in feet: 112 , 120, 175, 200 and 852. Before their revolutionary invention, Wilbur and Orville Wright were two ordinary brothers from the Midwest who possessed nothing more than natural talent, ambition, and imagination.

From an early age, the Wright brothers were fascinated by flight; they attributed their interest in aviation to a small helicopter toy their father brought back from his travels in France. While the Wright brothers were undoubtedly intelligent, neither of them ever earned his high school diploma or got married, since they were wedded to their work.

The Wright brothers wouldn't have known any success if it wasn't for their repeated and often painful failures. It took the self-taught engineers years and numerous attempts to get anywhere close to powered flight. The first coast-to-coast flight across the U.S. took almost three months.

Orville Wright once said, "If we all worked on the assumption that what is accepted as true is really true, there would be little hope of advance."

Michael Jordan

Michael Jordan missed more than nine thousand shots in his career and lost almost three hundred games. Twenty-six times, he was entrusted to take the winning shot and missed. But Jordan is still the most successful and talented basketball player in modern history, and the first athlete ever to become a billionaire.

"I've failed over and over and over again in my life. And that is why I succeed," he said once. "Some people want it to happen, some wish it would happen, others make it happen."

Charlie Chaplin

Charlie Chaplin's act was initially rejected by Hollywood studio chiefs because they felt it was a little too nonsensical (stupid) to ever sell. But Chaplin's life had very humble beginnings. His childhood was full of poverty and hardship. When he was fourteen, his mother was admitted to a mental asylum.

After Chaplin became a hit with the American audience during his sketch titled "A Night in an English Music Hall", he was then offered a motion picture contract. When his acting career began to rise, he was making around $1,200 per week. As he grew in his success, he then began making around $670,00 per year. Today, Chaplin is considered one of the most important figures in the history of the film industry. He once said, "To truly laugh, you must be able to take your pain, and play with it."

James Dyson

James Dyson invented a vacuum cleaner that is known around the world as the only one that doesn't lose suction. But it took Dyson 5,126 failures to finally get it right. Frustration with his Hoover launched him on a journey to create the world's first bagless vacuum cleaner at the age of thirty-six.

But no manufacturer or distributor in the U.K. would take on the revolutionary product, because it would disrupt the valuable market for replacement dust bags. Without skipping a beat, Dyson went to Japan, where he eventually won an industrial award. About three years later he was awarded his first U.S. patent. Today, he has a net worth of $5.8 billion. "Enjoy failure and learn from it," he said. "You can never learn from success."

Steven Spielberg

Steven Spielberg dropped out of college and was rejected three times from film school and was also a college dropout. He was also rejected twice for directing the James Bond franchise movies. But this successful entrepreneur does have a unique story on how his passion originally started. When he was a young teen he recorded family events using an 8-mm camera and continued that through high school. Later on, he got his breakthrough directing TV productions, which eventually led to him producing his own movies.

Today he is recognized as one of the best movie directors and producers of all time, with films like *Schindler's List*, *Jaws*, *Indiana Jones*, *Saving Private Ryan*, *Jurassic Park*, and *E.T.* "When I don't have a movie, I don't take a job just for the sake of working. I just sit it out until I find something I'm passionate about," he said once. "Whether in success or in failure, I'm proud of every single movie I've directed."

Albert Einstein

Albert Einstein, who developed the theory of relativity and had major influence in science, did not speak until age four or read until age seven. He was also expelled from school and eventually dropped out at age fifteen. It took Einstein nine years to get a job in academia; he had a poor memory and could not remember names, dates, or phone numbers.

Surprisingly, the FBI spied on Einstein for twenty-two years, listening to his phone calls and opening his letters, hoping to unmask him as a Soviet spy. But in 1921, he won the Nobel Prize for physics, and *Time* magazine named him its "Person of the Century." "Life is like riding a bicycle," he said. "To keep your balance, you must keep moving."

Attitude Principles To Consider

•   Striking out is just a sign that there is still plenty of room for growth and development.

•   Many Olympic athletes compete in a particular sport, but only three will receive medals. The rest do not get participation trophies.

•   Champions are developed in the hidden arena of their daily training. They are only honored on the podium.

•   There are many participants in life, but not many achievers.

•   Failure is not a sign of weakness, but not learning from it is.

•   Many people fail in life for simply not realizing how close they were to success when they gave up.

•   Whether you're ready or not, life will throw endless curveballs at you to strike you out; your attitude will position you correctly to swing for a homerun.

•   Your ability is what you're capable of doing, but your attitude determines how well you do it.

The attitude of these nine successful entrepreneurs makes them stand out from the average crowd. Why? In order to succeed greatly, you must be willing to fail greatly. Great success comes with a heavy price tag; those who are not willing to pay it will always be average.

As I write this, my son is finishing his last Little League baseball season before he goes into high school. I started filming his games when he was in first grade; it's amazing how much he has developed over those years. Early on, he and most of his fellow players would be playing "watch ball," not baseball, as they would continually watch the ball skim through the air hit the catcher's glove in the strike zone. Now, at fourteen, he knows better than to stand still and count those strikes.

Life is the same way. In the beginning of your journey, it's normal to take many strikes and even strike out. But as time goes by, you should be improving. If not, there's a problem with your attitude.

Remember that rewards will always cost you something in terms of failure, hardship, and rejection. But eventually, here and there, you will get homeruns. So, begin to reposition your attitude just like a baseball player would at the plate, and begin to focus on your dreams and goals, as you look forward to receiving your rewards in life.

Attitude Questions to Consider

1. Are you looking for a reward or a participation trophy?

2. Are you making things happen or watching them happen?

3. Are you standing still and playing watch-ball or swinging your bat and playing baseball?

Chapter 29

DISCOUNT PRICE OR FULL PRICE?

There's No Such Thing as a Free Lunch

If you want success, then figure out the price and pay it!

Here are a few reality-check questions to consider. Do you treat a rental car the same way you would your new car? Do you care just as much for a rental house as you would your own house?

In this chapter I want to focus on the vision that we set out for our life. I have never come across any successful individual who said they achieved success easily or comfortably.

I'm currently part of the John Maxwell Team, the world's largest coaching and mentoring program. I recently connected on social media with a young entrepreneur who has been a lifelong student of John C. Maxwell who wanted to be mentored, but didn't have the finances to join the program.

With my mentoring heart in full mode, I told him he could use my login information to take advantage of everything the John Maxwell online university has to offer. He wrote back, "Wow, thank you so much. I appreciate you offering your login, but I do not want to take advantage of you. Like John, he doesn't let anyone pay for their lunch. Well, neither do I. Meaning, I am forever grateful that you would offer the account info, but I need to earn it, and I will."

That made me check my own heart. I saw a slideshow of all of the books I had bought, all the conferences and seminars I had attended, and all the thousands of miles I had put on my car to get to them. I realized again there really *is* no such thing as a free lunch.

I have often heard it said, that many lottery winners go broke within the first five years, after obtaining all of their millions! So, one day I decided to do my own research. To my shock and surprise, I was able to discover a few traits that most of those lottery winners possessed. First, most of them earned less than $100k per year. Second, they had average jobs. And third, they went on a frantic spending spree without counting the full cost of what they were buying.

After doing my own homework on these multi-million dollar lottery winners, I came to these few conclusions:

1. Their average earning salary attitude and mindset did not allow them to properly handle or to wisely manage a large sum of money, with which they did not earn through their hard work effort.

2. They did not understand the true value and worth of all of their millions, which they have gained over night.

3. And finally, since they obtained this large amount of money like a free lunch, their attitude posture became like wreck less and irresponsible towards those millions, and that's why they spent most of the money and eventually went broke.

Your dreams have value; your vision has value; your potential has value; your purpose has value. And anything that has value will always have an expensive price tag. In the following section you will be introduced to an individual who understood the price of success.

THE LIFE ATTITUDE OF MAYA ANGELOU

Maya Angelou was an author, poet, actor, dancer, singer, songwriter, playwright, historian, teacher, and civil rights activist.

Her parents divorced when she was three years old, and she and her brother Bailey were sent to live with their paternal grandmother. When she was eight, Maya was raped by her mother's boyfriend. Angelou told her brother about it, then testified at her rapist's trial. She later learned he had been found beaten to death, apparently by her uncle's. Because of this, she stopped speaking in public for five years, believing her words had caused the murder. But over those five years of silence, Angelou developed her love of reading and literature.

When she was fourteen years old, she dropped out of school to become San Francisco's first African-American female cable car conductor. In the early 1950s she was a nightclub performer; she later moved to Egypt and lived there for about a year, working as an associate editor of the *Arab Observer*. In 1963, she moved to Ghana as an assistant administrator for the School of Music & Drama at the University of Ghana, and also worked as feature editor for the *African Review*.

Angelou helped Dr. Martin Luther King, Jr. in the civil rights movement as a for the Southern Christian

Leadership Conference. In 1973, she was nominated for a Tony Award in the category of Best Supporting Actress for her role in *Look Away*. In 1975, she was appointed to the Bicentennial Commission by President Gerald Ford, and also appeared in the television miniseries *Roots*.

She never went to college, but received more than fifty honorary degrees. She was also the first black female director and producer for 20th Century Fox.

Angelou mastered five languages besides English: French, Spanish, Italian, Arabic, and the West African language Fanti. She's the second poet in history to read a poem during the presidential inauguration. She also won a Grammy for an audio recording of it, *On The Pulse of Morning*, in the Best Spoken Word category.

Angelou taught classes in ethics, philosophy, theatre, theology, writing, and science. She was the first African-American female member of the Directors Guild of America. She won a total of three Grammy awards, and her screenplay, *Georgia, Georgia*, was the first original script by a black woman to be produced. Angelou was nominated for a Pulitzer Prize, and had her own line of Hallmark greeting cards. Over the course of her life, she published seven autobiographies, three books of essays, several books of poetry, and was presented the Presidential Medal of Freedom by Barack Obama in 2011.

Maya Angelou understood that success is not a handout.

Attitude Principles To Consider

•   Maya Angelou once said, "Try to be a rainbow in someone's cloud."

•   Any great achievement will require time and effort, but it's up to you if you are willing to invest the time and to pay that price.

•   Success does not come at a discount, so decide now how successful you want to become!

•   If you don't like something, try to change it! But if you can't change it, then try changing your attitude.

•   Your purpose in life is not to merely survive, but to succeed and to release your inner passion.

•   Be careful not to listen or to follow anyone who is not willing to show you their battle scars.

•   Anything that is original or authentic will always be costly and valuable.

•   The world desperately needs genuine and authentic people. So be an original, not a duplicate.

•   Do not allow your negative attitude to make you into a cheap knock-off Rolex watch, which is sold on a street corner for twenty bucks.

Maya Angelou's attitude allowed her to express herself through poetry, acting, dancing, singing and songwriting. She was able to take her struggles and bring life out of them. Likewise, let us also shift our attitude towards paying the full price for our success and happiness.

Attitude Questions to Consider

1. Are you willing to pay the price?
2. Are you always looking for shortcuts in life?
3. Are you looking for a purpose or a position?
4. Are you an original or a duplicate?

Chapter 30

ASHES OR BEAUTY?

The Power of Your Identity

One of the biggest tragedies in life is that many people choose to exist, rather than live! Discovering the power and the purpose of your identity is an essential task for each of us. If you do not discover why you were born, your life will be full of ashes instead of beauty.

An attitude of ashes takes what is whole, original, normal or valuable, and lets it disintegrate into dust. But an attitude of beauty takes what has been deformed, rejected, broken, or devastated, and transforms it into something new, fresh and beautiful.

We will have tragic and unpleasant situations that threaten to turn our life into ashes, but our attitude can turn that situation into something great and beautiful.

These are questions people often ask themselves:

1. Who am I? (Why was I born?)
2. Why am I here? (What is my purpose and destiny?)
3. What are my gifts, talents and abilities?
4. Where am I going? (What is my eternal destination?)

Its these four powerful questions of life that every living human being often thinks about, which places them on a continually search to discovering their inner identify of who they are and why they exist on this earth. But there are enormous amounts of hindrances in life that often times can derail us, keeping us from discovering our inner purpose and potential if we let them. So remember: You will never become who you were created to be until you are free from other people's perceptions of who they think you are or who you need to become.

We think of thieves as having evil motives, since they set out to steal something valuable that doesn't belong to them. That is true! But have you ever considered yourself to be a thief?

For example: If we have a negative or destructive attitude, we're robbing ourselves on a daily basis! When you have the attitude of ashes, you smudge out all of the hope of beauty for yourself!

Yes, the world is tough and rough and full of self-centered and egoistic individuals who are mainly concerned for their own well-being, but that should not become a justifiable excuse for you on why you are miserable and not living a life of fullness, but simply existing. And it would be a great tragedy to witness your potential dying without ever being discovered.

Your attitude defines who you are, the potential you have, and your purpose on this earth! Our next individual turned tragedy into triumph through his beautiful attitude.

THE LIFE ATTITUDE OF CHRISTOPHER REEVE

Christopher Reeve was an American actor, who played the iconic role of *Superman*, which made him a popular star. When he was nine years old, he found his passion for acting, and as he grew up he acted in many plays in school and later in theater.

His major Hollywood debut came in 1977, when the movie casting director for *Superman* placed a picture of Reeve on the list for audition, but the producers rejected it three times. By chance, Reeve got the main role after more than two hundred actors auditioned for it.

Reeve was the first actor to play the role of Superman in a movie, since it was born after the character was created in 1938. At the age of twenty-four, he became the youngest actor ever to be cast as Superman. Afterward, his fame grew and he appeared in *Superman* movie sequels.

In the late 1980s, Reeve took up equestrian sports and began training in order to participate in competitions. But on May 27, 1995, Reeve was thrown from his horse head-first during a show. The impact smashed the two upper vertebrae in his spine, leaving him completely paralyzed from the neck down and only able to breathe with assistance from a ventilator. Doctors gave him no more than a fifty-percent chance of survival.

Reeve, unable to speak at the time, mouthed to his wife Dana, "Maybe we should let me go." But his wife held onto him until the very end. Reeve eventually was able to master the art of talking between breaths from his ventilator. He also learned how to use a specialized wheelchair, which he commanded by blowing puffs of air into a straw-like control device.

In 1996, Reeve served as master of ceremonies at the Paralympic Games in Atlanta, and kept busy with countless speaking engagements. He and his wife Dana opened the Christopher and Dana Reeve Paralysis Resource Center, which was mainly devoted to teaching paralyzed people to live more independently; Reeve also served as a chairman of the American Paralysis Association.

In 1997, Reeve was awarded a star on the Hollywood Walk of Fame. "Some people are walking around with full use of their bodies and they're more paralyzed than I am," he once said. Reeve died of heart failure in 2004.

Life is full of irony. For example, when I was in school, I did not read any assigned books, since I honestly hated reading. I only started reading in college because I had to—and since I was paying for my own education and didn't want to waste the money. But now I am writing my second book and currently have a full library of over two hundred books, with the focus on leadership and personal development!

Reeve also knew irony: One of his last movie roles before the accident was playing a quadriplegic in the 1995 film *Above Suspicion*. But he rose to stardom by playing Superman—and after his accident, he accessed his own internal Superman attitude to give help and hope to others with physical disabilities.

Attitude Principles To Consider

•	Your character; your personality; your uniqueness; and your individuality is what defines your identity.

•	You cannot separate your identity from how you see and feel about yourself.

- Your attitude will either make you a super hero or a villain.
- The way you see yourself will determine through which type of prism you see everyone and everything.
- A negative attitude is like kryptonite; it can drain the life out of you.
- Your identity is like a hidden treasure that you need to discover and then present to the world.
- What people say about you reveals who they are; how you respond reveals who you are.
- Your thoughts about yourself today will determine who you become tomorrow.
- You will never achieve what you are unwilling to pursue.
- Christopher Reeve once said, "A hero is an ordinary individual who finds the strength to persevere and endure despite overwhelming obstacles."

Discovering your identity can transform you from a Clark Kent to a Superman. So, decide today to go into your phone booth (your mind) and begin to transform your ashes into beauty, as you present your unique identity to the whole world!

Your identity is as original and unique as your finger print. Every time you release and function in your purpose, gifting and potential, you always leave your visible identity imprint, just like a finger print. So, continue to function in your identity and continue to touch the lives of others, and in due time you will be called their superhero!

Attitude Questions to Consider

1. Do you see yourself in full color or in black and white?

2. Do you see yourself as a dorky Clark Kent or a as a powerful Superman (or Superwoman)?

3. Is your attitude making you a hero or a villain?

4. Have you discovered your identity and purpose?

Chapter 31

THE WORLD IS ALREADY FULL OF IT SO STOP COMPLAINING

Change Your Attitude to Change Your Life

I can sum up this whole book by saying, "Stop complaining about your problems and just move on with your life, since our world and society is already full of it and we are not looking for another contributor!"

The average person has up to 50,000 thoughts per day, and about 70 percent of them are negative. (Dang! Is this why I sometimes feel smoke coming out of my ears?) No wonder we so often feel tired or overwhelmed by the end of the day.

Attitude has specific laws and principles that cannot be avoided. Attitude is similar to weight loss, muscle toning, and personal development. In each of those areas, you have to have consistent, and continual growth. You don't just lose twenty pounds of fat with one day's worth of exercise, get toned muscles after two hours in the gym, or advance your personal knowledge in just one classroom session! Likewise, our attitude is a daily thing, not a one-time decision.

Here are ten Reality Checks that you can apply to your life that will keep you challenged and in a healthy balance.

Reality Check 1: Problems always were; always are; and always will be.

Reality Check 2: Pointing the finger at others is only letting them know you want your finger to be pulled. And that makes you look like an idiotic stinker. Just a thought!

Reality Check 3: This world and our society is already full of those who are full of it. Please don't become one of them!

Reality Check 4: Criticism, opposition, betrayal, backstabbing or mockery are simply tools that shape you into becoming a successful individual, if your attitude is properly aligned.

Reality Check 5: In order for you to succeed greatly, you must be willing to fail greatly. Great success comes with a heavy price tag and those who are not willing to pay the price will always be average.

Reality Check 6: There are NO handouts in life. You don't get something for nothing. Don't expect anything if you did nothing to earn it.

Reality Check 7: Your life is not an experiment; you were born to fulfill a specific purpose. But your attitude will determine whether you fulfill that purpose or not.

Reality Check 8: Your words can carry life and they can also carry death. Your words could be medicine or they could be poison.

Reality Check 9: What you tolerate, you cannot change.

Reality Check 10: God is not the problem! Your spouse is not the problem! Your children are not the problem! Your friends are not the problem! And your job is not the problem! You are the problem, so stop blaming the whole world and begin to re-adjust your attitude!

HOW MUCH BETTER OFF WILL THIS WORLD BE BECAUSE OF WHO YOU ARE?

Your mind is like a food bank which feeds your daily attitude. If you continually draw out candy, ice-cream, soda or beer, your attitude will not be healthy. But if you draw out vegetables, meats or juices, your attitude will be healthy. Just as "you are what you eat," you are the product of your own thinking.

For example, if you were to quit your job right now, would your managers and co-workers rejoice? Or would they be saddened and plead with you to stay? I want to challenge you to seriously consider how valuable you could be to your family; to your workplace; to your marriage or relationship; to your children; to our society; and to our world!

Again, your attitude is a reflection of what you believe about yourself. If you have discovered your identity, then your life choices will be mature and sound.

Remember, whatever you can conceive and believe, you can eventually achieve. This is also true with your attitude: If your attitude is right, then the world around you will become right. It won't become perfect, but because of your attitude, you will begin to see the best and brightest things the world has to offer. A healthy attitude is contagious! But don't wait to catch it from others; become a carrier.

Everyone wants to be happy, but happiness begins with your attitude. So don't sit around wasting your time waiting for someone to drop it into your lap. Likewise, if you want to achieve something great, then shift your attitude in that direction and stay focused all the way through. Because if you have the right attitude and constantly strive to give your best effort, eventually you will overcome your problems and discover that you are ready to embrace greater challenges.

Our world has a serious deficit of positivity, and often seems gray. But you can become a valuable asset, just like a box of colorful crayons, as you add greater value to everyone you encounter in your life. By being who God created you to be, and by realizing your potential, you will begin to add brighter colors into our grayish world.

Remember, you were given as a gift to this world. But it will depend upon you whether this world will be able to discover this gift and enjoy its full potential and benefits. How much better off will this world be because of who you are? How better off could our society become, just because you are part of it? How different would marriages and family relationships would be, if your attitude was right? And how much brighter would our world be because you chose to have the right mental attitude?

To wrap things up: Always remember that life is full of it, but there is always an antidote, and that is a changed attitude! As you re-adjust your attitude, you will begin to perceive, to interpret, and to evaluate *life* and all of its complexity in a whole different way. And since our world is already full of it, please do not become a contributor!

Change Your Attitude to Change Your Life!

Notes

Chapter 1 When Life Is Full of It

1. Nelson, T. *James 3:5-9 (NKJV)*. Retrieved from
    BibleGateway.com:
    https://www.biblegateway.com/passage/?search=James+3%3
    A5-9&version=NKJV

Chapter 2 Tombstone or Stepping Stone?

1. *Abraham Lincoln Biography*. Retrieved April 12, 2018, from The
    Biography.com website:
    https://www.biography.com/people/abraham-lincoln-9382540
2. Current, R. N. (1999, July 28). *Abraham Lincoln*. Retrieved from
    Encyclopædia Britannica:
    https://www.britannica.com/biography/Abraham-Lincoln

Chapter 3 Problem or Opportunity?

1. Smith, R. (2008, January 22). *Boll Weevil in Alabama*. Retrieved
    from The Encyclopedia of Alabama:
    http://www.encyclopediaofalabama.org/article/h-1436
2. Lorraine Boissoneault. (2017, May 31). *Why an Alabama Town Has
    a Monument Honoring the Most Destructive Pest in American
    History*. Retrieved from SMITHSONIAN.COM:
    https://www.smithsonianmag.com/history/agricultural-pest-
    honored-herald-prosperity-enterprise-alabama-180963506/
3. Mays, B. (1986, May 2). *From Hog Island To A Little Bit Of
    Heaven*. Retrieved from Orlando Sentinel:
    http://articles.orlandosentinel.com/1986-03-
    02/travel/0200290233_1_hog-island-paradise-island-paradise-
    resort
4. *Paradise Island*. Retrieved from Wikipedia.com:
    https://en.wikipedia.org/wiki/Paradise_Island
5. Editorial Staff. (2017, November 16). *52 Interesting Facts About
    Thomas Edison*. Retrieved from the FACT file:
    http://thefactfile.org/thomas-edison-facts/
6. (2017, August 4). *Thomas Edison Biography*. Retrieved from The
    Biography.com website:
    https://www.biography.com/people/thomas-edison-9284349

7. *Existing Businesses Started During The Great Depression*. Retrieved from Michael T. Chulak & Associates: http://www.mtclaw.com/businesses_started_during_depressio n.html

8. *The Statistics Portal*. Retrieved from The Statistics Portal: https://www.statista.com

Chapter 4 Complaint or Constraint?

1. *Biography of Nelson Mandela*. Retrieved from Nelson Mandela Foundation: https://www.nelsonmandela.org/content/page/biography

2. CNN Library. (2017, May 14). *Nelson Mandela Fast Facts*. Retrieved from CNN: https://www.cnn.com/2012/12/11/world/africa/nelson-mandela---fast-facts/index.html

3. Kharel, G. C. (2013, Dec 9). *80,000 People, 90 World Leaders Attend One of the Largest Funerals in History*. Retrieved from International Business Times, India Edition: https://www.ibtimes.co.in/80000-people-90-world-leaders-attend-one-of-the-largest-funerals-in-history-528583

Chapter 5 Monday or Moanday

1. *S. Truett Cathy*. Retrieved from Wikipedia: https://en.wikipedia.org/wiki/S._Truett_Cathy

2. Kim Bhasin. (2012, July 23). *Meet S. Truett Cathy, The 91-Year-Old Billionaire Behind Chick-fil-A*. Retrieved from Business Insider: http://www.businessinsider.com/meet-chick-fil-a-founder-s-truett-cathy-2012-7#cathy-first-got-into-the-restaurant-business-in-1946-after-serving-in-the-us-army-during-world-war-ii-1

3. Shana Lebowitz. (2015, May 30). *From the projects to a $2.3 billion fortune*. Retrieved from Business Insider: http://www.businessinsider.com/rags-to-riches-story-of-howard-schultz-2015-5

4. (2014, Dec 3). *Howard Schultz Biography*. Retrieved from The Biography.com website: https://www.biography.com/people/howard-schultz-21166227

5. (2017, May). *America's Best Employers*. Retrieved from Forbes: https://www.forbes.com/companies/starbucks/

6. *Amway by the Numbers*. Retrieved from Alticor Inc: https://www.amwayglobal.com/newsroom/facts-and-figures/

7. Morrison, J. (n.d.). *DeVos, Richard M.* Retrieved from Learning To Give: https://www.learningtogive.org/resources/devos-richard-m

8. *Amway.* Retrieved from Wikipedia: https://en.wikipedia.org/wiki/Amway

9. *Jay Van Andel.* Retrieved from Wikipedia: https://en.wikipedia.org/wiki/Jay_Van_Andel

10. Editors, TheFamousPeople.com. (2017, Sept 14). *John Paul DeJoria Biography.* Retrieved from TheFamousPeople.com: https://www.thefamouspeople.com/profiles/john-paul-dejoria-34087.php

11. *John Paul DeJoria.* Retrieved from Famous-Entrepreneurs.com: http://www.famous-entrepreneurs.com/john-paul-dejoria

12. *Shahid Khan Success Story.* Retrieved from SuccessStory.com: https://successstory.com/people/shahid-shad-khan

13. Ganguli, T. (2011, Dec 3). *Shahid Khan has true rags to riches American story.* Retrieved from Jacksonville.com: http://www.jacksonville.com/sports/football/jaguars/2011-12-03/story/shahid-khan-has-true-rags-riches-american-story

14. Kathleen Elkins. (2015, May 12). *From pumping gas to a $6 billion fortune.* Retrieved from BusinessInsider.com: http://www.businessinsider.com/rags-to-riches-story-of-forever-21-cofounders-2015-5

15. Berman, N. (2016). *10 Things You Didn't Know about Do Won Chang.* Retrieved from MoneyInc.com: http://moneyinc.com/do-won-chang-facts/

16. *Leonardo Del Story.* Retrieved from SuccessStory.com: https://successstory.com/people/leonardo-del-vecchio

17. Thompson, J. (2017, Jan 16). *Profile: Leonardo Del Vecchio, founder and chairman of Luxottica.* Retrieved from The Financial Times: https://www.ft.com/content/b10e0888-dbcd-11e6-9d7c-be108f1c1dce

18. (2015, April 15). *Sheldon Adelson Biography.* Retrieved from The Biography.com website: https://www.biography.com/people/sheldon-adelson-20956059

19. The Editors of Encyclopaedia Britannica. (n.d.). *Sheldon Adelson.* Retrieved from Encyclopædia Britannica, Inc.: https://www.britannica.com/biography/Sheldon-Adelson

20. Kim, L. (2015, April 14). *30 Surprising Facts About Billionaire Tycoon Larry Ellison.* Retrieved from Inc.com: https://www.inc.com/larry-kim/30-surprising-facts-about-billionaire-tycoon-larry-ellison.html

21. (2016, Feb 11). *Larry Ellison Biography*. Retrieved from The
    Biography.com website:
    https://www.biography.com/people/larry-ellison

Chapter 6 Commerical or Movie?

1. Arnold Schwarzenegger. (n.d.). *Bio*. Retrieved from
        Schwarzenegger.com: http://www.schwarzenegger.com/bio
2. Editor. (2015, June 12). *50 Interesting Facts About Arnold
    Schwarzenegger*. Retrieved from BOOMSbeat.com:
    http://www.boomsbeat.com/articles/21368/20150612/50-
    interesting-facts-arnold-schwarzenegger.htm
3. (2018, April 3). *Arnold Schwarzenegger Biography*. Retrieved from
    The Biography.com website:
    https://www.biography.com/people/arnold-schwarzenegger-
    9476355

Chapter 7 Mistakes of Lessons?

1. Krueger, A. (2010, Nov 16). *15 Life-Changing Inventions That Were
    Created By Mistake*. Retrieved from Business Insider:
    http://www.businessinsider.com/these-10-inventions-were-
    made-by-mistake-2010-11
2. Gaylord, P. C. (2012, Oct 5). *The 20 most fascinating accidental
    inventions*. Retrieved from The Christian Science Monitor:
    https://www.csmonitor.com/Technology/2012/1005/The-20-
    most-fascinating-accidental-inventions/Potato-chips
3. Sean Traynor. (2011, April). *Inventions that were Mistakes*.
    Retrieved from http://mag.amazing-kids.org/non-
    fiction/stories/inventions-that-were-mistakes/

Chapter 8 Pain or Passion?

1. (2018, Jan 19). *Ray Charles Biography*. Retrieved from The
    Biography.com website:
    https://www.biography.com/people/ray-charles-9245001
2. *Ray Charles Biography*. Retrieved from Advameg, Inc.:
    http://www.notablebiographies.com/Ch-Co/Charles-Ray.html

Chapter 9 Cat or Lion

1. (2018, March 21). *Oprah Winfrey Biography*. Retrieved from The Biography.com website: https://www.biography.com/people/oprah-winfrey-9534419
2. Lesley Messer and Luchina Fisher. (2014, Jan 28). *60 Facts About Oprah That You Probably Forgot*. Retrieved from ABC News Internet Ventures: https://abcnews.go.com/Entertainment/60-facts-oprah-forgot/story?id=22269267
3. CNN Library. (2018, Mar 19). *Oprah Winfrey Fast Facts*. Retrieved from Cable News Network: https://www.cnn.com/2013/08/05/us/oprah-winfrey-fast-facts/index.html

Chapter 10 Contract or Commitment?

1. (2016, Oct 17). *John Wooden Biography*. Retrieved from The Biography.com website: https://www.biography.com/people/john-wooden-21369183
2. Penner, M. (2009, Oct 14). *99 things about John Wooden*. Retrieved from Los Angeles Times: http://articles.latimes.com/2009/oct/14/sports/sp-john-wooden14
3. The Gale Group, I. (n.d.). *Wooden, John*. Retrieved from Encyclopedia.com: https://www.encyclopedia.com/people/sports-and-games/sports-biographies/john-r-wooden

Chapter 11 Division or Multiplication?

1. (2018, Feb 27). *Helen Keller Biography*. Retrieved from The Biography.com website: https://www.biography.com/people/helen-keller-9361967
2. Raga, S. (2016, June 27). *10 Things You Might Not Know About Helen Keller*. Retrieved from Mental Floss: http://mentalfloss.com/article/81472/10-things-you-might-not-know-about-helen-keller

Chapter 12 Revenge or Release?

1. (2014, Dec 1). *Louis Zamperini Biography*. Retrieved from The Biography.com website: https://www.biography.com/people/louis-zamperini
2. richardgreen2014 (2014, Dec 24). *Louis Zamperini: The Story of a True American Hero*. Retrieved from https://unwritten-

record.blogs.archives.gov/2014/12/24/louis-zamperini-the-
story-of-a-true-american-hero/

3. (2014, Dec 24). *Louis Zamperini: 10 Incredible Facts About the
"Unbroken" Hero*. Retrieved from Haymarket Media, Inc.:
https://www.medicalbag.com/grey-matter/louis-zamperini-10-
incredible-facts-about-the-unbroken-hero/article/472878/

Chapter 13 Fear or Faith?

1. (2017, April 27). *Mary Kay Ash Biography*. Retrieved from The
Biography.com website:
https://www.biography.com/people/mary-kay-ash-197044

2. *About*. Retrieved from Mary Kay: https://www.marykay.com/en-
us/about-mary-kay/company-and-founder/about-mary-kay-ash

3. (2016, Jan 8). *25 Amazing Facts About Mary Kay (the Woman and
her Company)*. Retrieved from SPAN Enterprises LLC:
http://blog.unitwise.com/2016/01/25-amazing-facts-about-
mary-kay-woman.html

Chapter 14 Greed or Need?

1. (n.d.). *Goodwill Industries*. Retrieved from Wikipedia:
https://en.wikipedia.org/wiki/Goodwill_Industries

2. *History*. Retrieved from Goodwill Corporate:
http://www.goodwillworks.org/History

3. *Our Success Stories*. Retrieved from Goodwill Industries
International, Inc.: http://www.goodwill.org/annual-report/

4. *History of the Salvation Army*. Retrieved from The Salvation Army
USA: https://www.salvationarmyusa.org/usn/history-of-the-
salvation-army/

5. Ashley Grossman. (2017, May 12). *Eight fun facts you didn't know
about The Salvation Army*. Retrieved from The Salvation
Army: http://salvationarmynorth.org/2017/05/eight-fun-facts-
you-didnt-know-about-the-salvation-army/

6. *William Booth Biography*. Retrieved from Biography Online:
https://www.biographyonline.net/spiritual/william-booth.html

Chapter 15 Bitter or Better?

1. *MADD History*. Retrieved from MADD:
https://www.madd.org/history/

2. (2016, May 23). *Candy Lightner Biography*. Retrieved from The Biography.com website: https://www.biography.com/people/candy-lightner-21173669
3. Prof. David J. Hanson, P. (n.d.). *Candy Lightner (Candace Lightner): Founder of MADD*. Retrieved from Alcohol Problems and Solutions: https://www.alcoholproblemsandsolutions.org/candy-lightner/

Chapter 16 Fragile or Firm?

1. *FDR Biography*. Retrieved from Franklin D. Roosevelt Library & Museum: https://fdrlibrary.org/fdr-biography
2. Frank Freidel (The Editors of Encyclopaedia Britannica). (2000, Jan 12). *Franklin D. Roosevelt*. Retrieved from Encyclopaedia Britannica: https://www.britannica.com/biography/Franklin-D-Roosevelt
3. Greenspan, J. (2015, April 8). *9 Things You May Not Know About Franklin D. Roosevelt*. Retrieved from https://www.history.com/news/9-things-you-may-not-know-about-franklin-d-roosevelt

Chapter 17 Trials or Triumphs?

1. *Nick Vujicic BIO*. Retrieved from Life Without Limbs Inc: https://www.lifewithoutlimbs.org/about-nick/bio/
2. Kumar, A. (2012, Sept 3). *Nick Vujicic on Why God Made Him Limbless*. Retrieved from The Christian Post: https://www.christianpost.com/news/nick-vujicic-on-why-god-made-him-limbless-80996/
3. James, S. D. (2015, June 17). *Born without limbs star inspires with courage and trust in God*. Retrieved from TODAY: https://www.today.com/health/born-without-limbs-star-nick-vujicic-lives-courage-t26796

Chapter 18 Employment or Deployment?

1. History.com Staff. (2010). *John D. Rockefeller*. Retrieved from History.com: https://www.history.com/topics/john-d-rockefeller
2. Gelderman, C. W. (2018, April 26). *Henry Ford*. Retrieved from Encyclopædia Britannica: https://www.britannica.com/biography/Henry-Ford

3. The Editors of Encyclopaedia Britannica. (2017, Feb 23). *Ray Kroc*. Retrieved from Encyclopædia Britannica: https://www.britannica.com/biography/Ray-Kroc

4. *Kirk Kerkorian Biography*. Retrieved from Notable Biographies: http://www.notablebiographies.com/supp/Supplement-Ka-M/Kerkorian-Kirk.html

5. *Business Leaders Biography of David Murdock*. Retrieved from 4-Traders: http://www.4-traders.com/business-leaders/David-Murdock-1416/biography/

6. (2018, April 3). *Richard Branson Biography*. Retrieved from The Biography.com website: https://www.biography.com/people/richard-branson-9224520

7. Press, T. A. (2011, Oct 18). *Billionaire philanthropist and financier Carl Lindner Jr dead at 92*. Retrieved from NBCNews.com: http://www.nbcnews.com/id/44941421/ns/us_news-giving/t/billionaire-philanthropist-financier-carl-lindner-jr-dead/

8. (2014, April 9). *James Clark Biography*. Retrieved from The Biography.com website: https://www.biography.com/people/james-clark-9542204

9. The Editors of Encyclopaedia Britannica. (2017, Aug 21). *François Pinault*. Retrieved from Encyclopædia Britannica: https://www.britannica.com/biography/Francois-Pinault

10. Ethan Trex. (2010, Oct 5). *11 High School Dropouts Who Found Success Anyway*. Retrieved from MentalFloss.com: http://mentalfloss.com/article/25990/11-high-school-dropouts-who-found-success-anyway

11. the Editors of Publications International, L. (2007, Sept 11). *15 Notable People Who Dropped Out of School*. Retrieved from HowStuffWorks.com: https://people.howstuffworks.com/15-notable-people-who-dropped-out-of-school1.htm

Chapter 19 Foe or Friend?

1. Pallardy, R. (2018, April 21). *Oskar Schindler*. Retrieved from Encyclopædia Britannica: https://www.britannica.com/biography/Oskar-Schindler

2. (2016, July 22). *Oskar Schindler Biography*. Retrieved from The Biography.com website: https://www.biography.com/people/oskar-schindler

3. New World Encyclopedia writers and editors. (2017, Mar 24). *Corrie ten Boom*. Retrieved from New World Encyclopedia:

http://www.newworldencyclopedia.org/entry/Corrie_ten_Boo
m

4. (2015, April 8). *Corrie ten Boom Biography*. Retrieved from The
Biography.com website:
https://www.biography.com/people/corrie-ten-boom-
21358155

Chapter 20 Death or Life?

1. Nelson, T. (n.d.). *Proverbs 18:21 (NKJV)*. Retrieved from
BibleGateway.com:
https://www.biblegateway.com/passage/?search=Proverbs+18
%3A21&version=NKJV

2. Amadio, A. J. (2018, Mar 28). *Aristotle*. Retrieved from
Encyclopædia Britannica:
https://www.britannica.com/biography/Aristotle

3. Bermosa, N. (2012, Aug 13). *30 Interesting Facts About Aristotle,
the Great Greek Philosopher*. Retrieved from
Biographies.Knoji.com: https://biographies.knoji.com/30-
interesting-facts-about-aristotle-the-great-greek-philosopher/

4. (2017, Nov 16). *Aristotle Biography*. Retrieved from The
Biography.com website:
https://www.biography.com/people/aristotle-9188415

5. Cohen, J. (2013, Jan 28). *7 Surprising Facts About Joan of Arc*.
Retrieved from History.com:
https://www.history.com/news/history-lists/7-surprising-facts-
about-joan-of-arc

6. (2018, Feb 27). *Joan of Arc Biography*. Retrieved from The
Biography.com website:
https://www.biography.com/people/joan-of-arc-9354756

7. (2018, Mar 9). *Mahatma Gandhi Biography*. Retrieved from The
Biography.com website:
https://www.biography.com/people/mahatma-gandhi-9305898

8. History.com Staff. (2010). *Mohandas Gandhi*. Retrieved from
History.com: https://www.history.com/topics/mahatma-gandhi

9. Rodgers, G. (2018, Jan 8). *20 Facts About the Life of Mahatma
Gandhi, Father of Modern India*. Retrieved from
TripSavvy.com: https://www.tripsavvy.com/interesting-
gandhi-facts-1458248

10. John Lukacs, Alan Bullock, Baron Bullock and Others (See All
Contributors). (2018, April 23). *Adolf Hitler*. Retrieved from
Encyclopædia Britannica:
https://www.britannica.com/biography/Adolf-Hitler

11. Saad, M. R. (2016, Feb 14). *20 Interesting Facts About Hitler.* Retrieved from WarHistoryOnline.com: https://www.warhistoryonline.com/featured/36-interesting-facts-about-hitler.html/2

12. (2017, Aug 5). *Adolf Hitler Biography.* Retrieved from The Biography.com website: https://www.biography.com/people/adolf-hitler-9340144

13. (2017, April 27). *Alexander the Great Biography.* Retrieved from The Biography.com website: https://www.biography.com/people/alexander-the-great-9180468

14. II, T. (2016, Mar 24). *25 Unusual Facts About Alexander The Great.* Retrieved from list25.com: https://list25.com/25-unusual-facts-about-alexander-the-great/

15. (2010, April 28). *TRANSLATOR WILLIAM TYNDALE STRANGLED AND BURNED.* Retrieved from Christianity.com: https://www.christianity.com/church/church-history/timeline/1501-1600/translator-william-tyndale-strangled-and-burned-11629961.html

16. (2018). *William Tyndale.* Retrieved from Encyclopedia of World Biography: https://www.encyclopedia.com/people/philosophy-and-religion/protestant-christianity-biographies/william-tyndale

17. Pettinger, T. (2014, Aug 5). *William Tyndale Biography.* Retrieved from www.biographyonline.net: https://www.biographyonline.net/spiritual/william-tyndale.html

18. *Shakespeare Facts: Read Facts About William Shakespeare.* Retrieved from NoSweatShakespeare.com: https://www.nosweatshakespeare.com/resources/shakespeare-facts/

19. *Facts about William Shakespeare.* Retrieved from BiographyOnline.net: https://www.biographyonline.net/poets/facts-shakespeare.html

20. *poet William Shakespeare.* Retrieved from Poets.org: https://www.poets.org/poetsorg/poet/william-shakespeare

21. (2017, Aug 5). *William Shakespeare Biography.* Retrieved from The Biography.com website: https://www.biography.com/people/william-shakespeare-9480323

22. Nelson, T. *John 14:6 (NKJV).* Retrieved from BibleGateway.com:

https://www.biblegateway.com/passage/?search=John+14%3
A6&version=NKJV

Chapter 21 Dam or River?

1. History.com Staff. (2010). *Hoover Dam*. Retrieved from
     History.com: https://www.history.com/topics/hoover-dam
2. ARBEITER, M. (2015, Sept 10). *14 Powerful Facts About the*
     Hoover Dam. Retrieved from Mental Floss:
     http://mentalfloss.com/article/67916/14-powerful-facts-about-
     hoover-dam
3. *BIOGRAPHY*. Retrieved from MotherTeresa.org:
     http://www.motherteresa.org/biography.html
4. Legacy Staff. (2016). *20 FACTS ABOUT MOTHER TERESA*.
     Retrieved from Legacy.com:
     http://www.legacy.com/news/explore-history/article/20-facts-
     about-mother-teresa
5. (2018, Feb 27). *Mother Teresa Biography*. Retrieved from The
     Biography.com website:
     https://www.biography.com/people/mother-teresa-9504160

Chapter 22 Destruction or Construction?

1. Carson, D. L. (2018, March 29). *Martin Luther King, Jr.* Retrieved
     from Encyclopædia Britannica:
     https://www.britannica.com/biography/Martin-Luther-King-Jr
2. Library, C. (2018, April 4). *Martin Luther King Jr. Fast Facts*.
     Retrieved from CNN.com:
     https://www.cnn.com/2013/01/17/us/martin-luther-king-jr-
     fast-facts/index.html
3. (2018, Jan 18). *Martin Luther King Jr. Biography*. Retrieved from
     The Biography.com website:
     https://www.biography.com/people/martin-luther-king-jr-
     9365086

Chapter 23 Give Up or Grow Up?

1. Greenspan, J. (2014, April 9). *10 Things You May Not Know About*
     Winston Churchill. Retrieved from History.com:
     https://www.history.com/news/10-things-you-may-not-know-
     about-winston-churchill
2. (2017, Nov 20). *Winston Churchill Biography*. Retrieved from The
     Biography.com website:

https://www.biography.com/people/winston-churchill-9248164

3. Nicholas, H. G. (2018, Jan 3). *Winston Churchill*. Retrieved from Encyclopædia Britannica: https://www.britannica.com/biography/Winston-Churchill

Chapter 24 Me or We?

1. *Emergency workers killed in the September 11 attacks*. Retrieved from Wikipedia: https://en.wikipedia.org/wiki/Emergency_workers_killed_in_the_September_11_attacks

Chapter 25 Follower or Leader?

1. *The John Maxwell Team*. Retrieved from JohnMaxwellTeam.com website: http://johnmaxwellteam.com

Chapter 26 Criticize or Analyze?

1. Kim, L. (2015, April 29). *31 Surprising Facts About Walt Disney*. Retrieved from Inc.com: https://www.inc.com/larry-kim/31-surprising-facts-about-walt-disney.html
2. Stacy Conradt. (2016, Dec 15). *15 Intriguing Facts About Walt Disney*. Retrieved from Mental Floss: http://mentalfloss.com/article/89835/15-intriguing-facts-about-walt-disney
3. (2017, Aug 7). *Walt Disney Biography*. Retrieved from The Biography.com website: https://www.biography.com/people/walt-disney-9275533
4. Kim, L. (2015, Mar 25). *43 Surprising Facts About Steve Jobs*. Retrieved from Inc.com: https://www.inc.com/larry-kim/43-surprising-facts-about-steve-jobs.html
5. CNN Library. (2017, May 8). *Steve Jobs Fast Facts*. Retrieved from CNN.com: https://www.cnn.com/2013/08/23/us/steve-jobs-fast-facts/index.html
6. (2018, May 7). *Steve Jobs Biography*. Retrieved from The Biography.com website: https://www.biography.com/people/steve-jobs-9354805
7. Olivia Pasquarelli. (n.d.). *60 facts about the wonderful world of Dr. Seuss*. Retrieved from Cbc.ca: http://www.cbc.ca/books/60-facts-about-the-wonderful-world-of-dr-seuss-1.4557340

8. (2018, Feb 6). *Dr. Seuss Biography*. Retrieved from The Biography.com website: https://www.biography.com/people/dr-seuss-9479638

9. Kim, L. (2016, April 6). *25 Surprising Facts About Billionaire Entrepreneur Bill Gates*. Retrieved from Inc.com: https://www.inc.com/larry-kim/25-surprising-facts-about-billionaire-entrepreneur-bill-gates.html

10. (2018, April 30). *Bill Gates Biography*. Retrieved from The Biography.com website: https://www.biography.com/people/bill-gates-9307520

11. Andrew LaSane. (2016, April 7). *15 Sweet Facts About Hershey's*. Retrieved from Mental Floss: http://mentalfloss.com/article/67616/15-sweet-facts-about-hersheys

12. (2017, April 27). *Milton Hershey Biography*. Retrieved from The Biography.com website: https://www.biography.com/people/milton-hershey-9337133

13. (2017, Dec 7). *Harrison Ford Biography*. Retrieved from The Biography.com website: https://www.biography.com/people/harrison-ford-9298701

14. Frank Pallotta. (2014, April 14). *Harrison Ford Explains How He Went From Full-Time Carpenter To Han Solo In 'Star Wars'*. Retrieved from Business Insider: http://www.businessinsider.com/harrison-ford-reddit-ama-from-carpenter-to-han-solo-in-star-wars-2014-4

Chapter 27 Skunk or Perfume?

1. *Sam Walton*. Retrieved from Entrepreneur.com: https://www.entrepreneur.com/article/197560

2. The Editors of Encyclopaedia Britannica. (2018, Mar 29). *Sam Walton*. Retrieved from Encyclopædia Britannica: https://www.britannica.com/biography/Sam-Walton

3. (2015, Mar 26). *Sam Walton Biography*. Retrieved from The Biography.com website: https://www.biography.com/people/sam-walton-9523270

Chapter 28 Strikeout or Homerun?

1. *Biography*. Retrieved from BabeRuth.com: http://www.baberuth.com/biography/

2. Cliff Corcoran. (2013, July 11). *99 Cool Facts About Babe Ruth*. Retrieved from Sports Illustrated:

https://www.si.com/mlb/strike-zone/2013/07/12/99-cool-facts-about-babe-ruth

3. (2017, April 27). *Babe Ruth Biography*. Retrieved from The Biography.com website: https://www.biography.com/people/babe-ruth-9468009

4. (2018). *Soichiro Honda Biography: A Great History of Japanese Car Manufacturer*. Retrieved from Astrum People website: https://astrumpeople.com/soichiro-honda-biography-a-great-history-of-japanese-car-manufacturer/

5. *Soichiro Honda Biography*. Retrieved from NotableBiographies.com: http://www.notablebiographies.com/He-Ho/Honda-Soichiro.html

6. Flessa, M.-E. (2017, Feb 2). *Colonel Sanders Trivia: 73 fascinating facts about the KFC founder!* Retrieved from UselessDaily.com: https://www.uselessdaily.com/food/colonel-sanders-trivia-73-fascinating-facts-about-the-kfc-founder/

7. (2017, April 27). *Colonel Harland Sanders Biography*. Retrieved from The Biography.com website: https://www.biography.com/people/colonel-harland-sanders-12353545

8. Alchin, L. (2014, July 1). *Wright Brothers Facts*. Retrieved from American-Historama.org: http://www.american-historama.org/1881-1913-maturation-era/wright-brothers-facts.htm

9. Crouch, T. D. (2017, Nov 13). *Wright brothers*. Retrieved from Encyclopædia Britannica: https://www.britannica.com/biography/Wright-brothers

10. (2015, May 27). *47 Facts About Michael Jordan, The Greatest Basketball Player Of All Time*. Retrieved from BoomsBeat.com: http://www.boomsbeat.com/articles/20941/20150527/42-facts-michael-jordan-greatest-basketball-player-time.htm

11. (2018, Jan 18). *Michael Jordan Biography*. Retrieved from The Biography.com website: https://www.biography.com/people/michael-jordan-9358066

12. Pirnia, G. (2018, April 16). *10 Enduring Facts About Charlie Chaplin*. Retrieved from Mental Floss website: http://mentalfloss.com/article/94491/10-enduring-facts-about-charlie-chaplin

13. (2017, April 27). *Charlie Chaplin Biography*. Retrieved from The Biography.com website: https://www.biography.com/people/charlie-chaplin-9244327

14. EFFRON, K. L. (2013, Aug 19). *Sir James Dyson: 7 Things You Didn't Know About Suction King*. Retrieved from ABC News website: https://abcnews.go.com/Business/sir-james-dyson-things-suction-king/story?id=19985903

15. The Editors of Encyclopaedia Britannica. (2018, May 1). *Sir James Dyson*. Retrieved from Encyclopædia Britannica: https://www.britannica.com/biography/James-Dyson

16. *Quick Facts*. Retrieved from GraceLand.com website: https://www.graceland.com/elvis/biography/quickfacts.aspx

17. (2018, April 5). *Elvis Presley Biography*. Retrieved from The Biography.com website: https://www.biography.com/people/elvis-presley-9446466

18. *30 Facts About Your Favorite Steven Spielberg Movies*. Retrieved from Mental Floss website: http://mentalfloss.com/article/71736/30-facts-about-your-favorite-steven-spielberg-movies

19. Barson, M. (2018, May 2). *Steven Spielberg*. Retrieved from Encyclopædia Britannica: https://www.britannica.com/biography/Steven-Spielberg

20. Editorial Staff. (2018, Feb 8). *50 Interesting Facts About Albert Einstein*. Retrieved from TheFactFile.org website: http://thefactfile.org/albert-einstein-facts/

21. (2017, Dec 20). *Albert Einstein Biography*. Retrieved from The Biography.com website: https://www.biography.com/people/albert-einstein-9285408

Chapter 29 Discount Price or Full Price?

1. Krystie Lee Yandoli and Justin Carissimo. (2014, May 28). *50 Facts Everyone Should Know About Maya Angelou*. Retrieved from BuzzFeed.com website: https://www.buzzfeed.com/krystieyandoli/50-facts-everyone-should-know-about-maya-angelou?utm_term=.tbgm50Nnv#.oi4WwDY0q

2. (2018, Feb 27). *Maya Angelou Biography*. Retrieved from The Biography.com website: https://www.biography.com/people/maya-angelou-9185388

3. The Editors of Encyclopaedia Britannica. (2018, Mar 29). *Maya Angelou*. Retrieved from Encyclopædia Britannica: https://www.britannica.com/biography/Maya-Angelou

Chapter 30 Ashes or Beauty?

1. *Biography*. Retrieved from Chrisreevehomepage.com website:
    http://www.chrisreevehomepage.com/biography.html
2. (2016, Jan 22). *50 Interesting Facts About Christopher Reeve – The Fan-Favorite Superman*. Retrieved from BoomsBeat.com website:
    http://www.boomsbeat.com/articles/106037/20160122/50-interesting-facts-christopher-reeve-%E2%80%93-fan-favorite-superman.htm
3. (2014, Dec 29). *Christopher Reeve Biography*. Retrieved from The Biography.com website:
    https://www.biography.com/people/christopher-reeve-9454130

Chapter 31 The World Is Already Full of It So Stop Complaining

1. Marano, H. E. (2001, July 1). *Depression Doing the Thinking*. Retrieved from Psychology Today website:
    https://www.psychologytoday.com/us/articles/200107/depression-doing-the-thinking

ABOUT THE AUTHOR

Stan Belyshev is an entrepreneur, author, life coach, speaker and trainer. He is part of The John Maxwell Team, which is compromised of thousands of coaches and mentors from around the world. Personal growth & development has been my inner drive for many years. I like to live by this personal motto: *"How many people will be better off because of who I'm and what value I could add to their life."*

Printed in Great Britain
by Amazon